Collector's Guide to

Owens Pottery

(As made by The J. B. Owens Pottery Company of Zanesville, Ohio)

By Frank L. Hahn

Golden Era Publications

Credits:

Color Photography - Ken Yamada and Keiko Hahn

Supplemental Research - Allan and Karen Nester

Computer Work - Keiko Hahn and Ray Weber

Photo Processing - Dodds, Lima, Ohio and Colour Klassic Pro Lab, Delphos, Ohio

Published By

Golden Era Publications

(A DIVISION OF GREEN GATE ENTERPRISES)

P. O. Box 934

Lima, Ohio 45802

Additional copies may be ordered from the above.

Printed in the U.S.A. by Image Graphics

PREFACE

The J. B. Owens Pottery Company was a principle maker of pottery in Zanesville, Ohio. The other two best known makers were Roseville and Weller. While much has been written about these two, nothing definitive has ever been written about J. B. Owens and his pottery, even though Owens himself was an influential citizen of Zanesville and his pottery was a major employer at that time.

This is not too surprising since some of the events which happened during Owens' time in business are not entirely clear, and extensive efforts to locate Owens' pottery catalogs and old literature have been unsuccessful. Accordingly, this book has been assembled through research in old Zanesville newspapers, in old pottery trade magazines, from some written accounts, through the examination of numerous pieces of Owens pottery, and with the help of many Owens collectors.

Great care has been taken to ensure that the information contained herein is as accurate as possible, but there remains the realization that the subsequent discovery of old catalogs or presently unknown reference materials could provide even more comprehensive information.

Research will be continued, and, if enough new information is uncovered, another book will be published. Anyone who can add to the information herein, or has interesting examples of Owens' pottery not well covered, is urged to contact the author at the address on page two.

DEDICATION

This book is dedicated to my father and mother, both long deceased, who had no idea during their lifetimes that I would ever write a book on anything.

And to my wife, Keiko, whose patience with me in the writing of this book has been nothing short of amazing.

Frank L. Hahn

ACKNOWLEDGMENTS

The cooperation and encouragement toward writing this book, and the providing of pictures by many collectors of Owens pottery is greatly appreciated. I am especially indebted to the following:

Claudia Aaron	Robert C. Friedrich	Armand F. Miranda
Tom Andrews	Mike Nickel	Bill Neidlinger
Blaine Andrus	Wayne Gage	Bill Noonan
Joe A. Bailey, Sr.	Ken Galvas	Ron & Judy Owens
W. Clare and Lucille Barnett	David Edwin Gifford	Nancy J. Perrin
Bill and Madeleine Beck	D. W. Gilman	David L. Powell
Bob and Kathy Bettinger	Rebecca T. Haller	Ted and Pat Sallaz
Betty Blair	Jerry Harrington	Sam and Faydelle Schott
Joan Bungum	Herb and Marti Hawk	Richard A. Sherman
Virginia Buxton	Roy Higgins	Marv and Jen Stofft
Jim Campbell	Ralph and Jackie Hoffman	John J. Sullivan
John Canfield	Beth Hylen	Mitch Taylor
Diane and Mike Cole	Martin Ives	Graham Owens Weaver
Patricia Crane	Vera Kaufman	Mark Weeks
Dorothy Daniel	Steve Lones	Lynn M. Welker
Karl A. Davis	Si Lambert	Claude Williamson
Hilda Dietrich	John McCarthy	John C. Williamson
Dick Downey	Ann McDonald	Joe and Gretchen Wirtz
Mr. & Mrs. H. B. Drew	Merry Jo McFarlane	Russell D. and Jo Ann Wright
Mark & Linda Ervin	Dann McKee	Allan Wunsch
Keith Evans	Clark and Vickie McLean	Hilda E. Yinger
Jim and Jennifer Fell	Mose Mesre	Zanesville Art Center
Bob Flanders	Cort and Chris Michener	

My deepest gratitude goes to anyone not mentioned who helped me in any way.

CONTENTS

PAGE

ACKNOWLEDGEMENTS 4

ADVERTISING AND TRADE MAGAZINE INFORMATION 19

ARTISTS AND THEIR MONOGRAMS AND SIGNATURES 28

BIOGRAPHY OF J. B. OWENS 9

BIBLIOGRAPHY 6

BLACK AND WHITE PICTURES AND ILLUSTRATIONS INDEX 128

CATALOGS AND LITERATURE 19

COLOR SECTION WITH INFORMATION ON OWENS' POTTERY LINES 33

ABORIGINE 34
ALPINE 36
AMERICAN AWAJA WARE (LWOP) 60
AQUA VERDI 38
ART NOUVEAU 39
ART VELLUM 40
BRUSHMODEL LOTUS (LWOP) 60
CORONA 41
CORONA ANIMALS 42
CORONA GREEN (LWOP) 60
CREAMWARE* 44
CYRANO 45
DELFT 46
EMBOSSED LOTUS* 47
FEROZA 48
GREEN WARE* 49
GUN METAL (LWOP).....................61
HENRI DEUX 52
JASPER ART (LWOP).....................61
JEWELED* 54
KORINA (LWOP) 62
LIGHTWEIGHT* 56
LINES WITHOUT PICTURES (LWOP) 60
LOTUS 64
MAJOLICA FINISH 70
MATT GREEN 72
MATT UTOPIAN 74

METAL DEPOSIT 77
MISSION POTTERY 78
MONOCHROME ART 81
MULTI-COLOR BLENDS (LWOP) 62
OLD COPPER (LWOP) 62
ONYX 82
OPALESCE 84
OPALESCE INLAID 85
OPALESCE UTOPIAN 86
ORIENTAL 88
PARCHMENT LOTUS (LWOP).............62
PERSIAN (LWOP) 63
POSTER 91
RAINBOW BRONZE (LWOP).............63
RED FLAME (LWOP) 63
RUSTIC 92
SEMI-GLAZED ETCHED 93
SILVER OVERLAY UTOPIAN
        AND LIGHTWEIGHT 94
SOUDANEZE 95
SUNBURST 96
SYLVAN GREEN 97
TILE 98
TRANSFER* 99
UNIDENTIFIED AS TO LINE 100
UTOPIAN 106
VENETIAN 126

(LWOP) Lines Without Pictures.

COMPANY MARKS ON OWENS' POTTERY 24

DEDICATION 4

DISTRIBUTION 18

EXPOSITIONS AND EXHIBITS 20

IDENTIFICATION OF OWENS' ART POTTERY 16

LINE NAME MARKINGS 27

OTHER NUMBERS AND LETTERS 17

OWENS' POTTERY 14

POTTERS, CHEMISTS AND OTHERS AT OWENS 21

PREFACE 3

SHAPES AND SHAPE NUMBERS 17

YEARS LINES WERE INTRODUCED 23

BIBLIOGRAPHY

Zanesville Art Pottery in Color by Purviance and Schneider - Copyright: 1968

Roseville Pottery: First Series by Sharon and Bob Huxford - Copyright: 1976

Weller Pottery by Sharon and Bob Huxford - Copyright: 1979

Roseville Pottery: Second Series by Sharon and Bob Huxford - Copyright: 1980

Art Pottery of America by Lucile Henzke - Copyright: 1982

Dictionary Guide to United States Pottery and Porcelain by Jenny B. Derwich & Dr. Mary Latos - Copyright: 1984

Art Pottery of the United States by Paul Evans - Copyright: 1987

All About Weller by Ann Gilbert McDonald - Copyright: 1989

Marks of American Potters by Edwin Atlee Barber - 1904

The Guide to Brush-McCoy Pottery by Martha and Steve Sanford - Copyright: 1992

Kovels' American Art Pottery by Ralph and Terry Kovel - Copyright: 1993

Old Zanesville Evening Signal and Zanesville Daily Courier Newspapers.

Articles and Advertisements from old trade magazines such as Brick, Brick and Clay Record, China Glass and Lamps, China Glass and Pottery Review, Clay Record, Clay Worker, Crockery and Glass Journal, Glass and Pottery World, etc.

Some of the black and white pictures and illustrations were taken from old trade magazines in the collections of The Library of Congress, Washington, D. C.

Microfilm of old trade magazines in the Rakow Library, Corning Museum of Glass, Corning, New York, was used extensively.

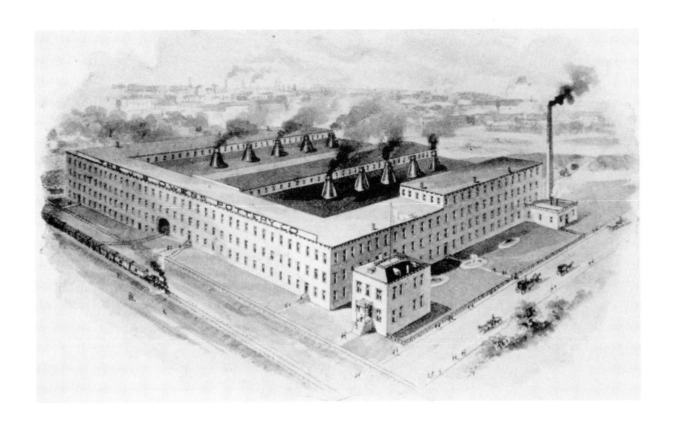

From the "Industrial, Mercantile and Picturesque Zanesville" by Thos. W. Lewis. Copyright, 1895.

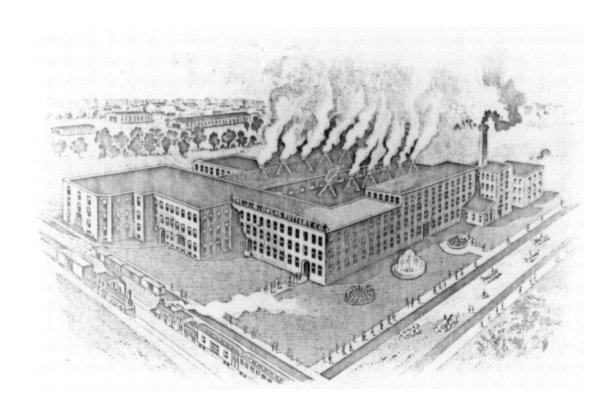

From the December, 1901, Issue of China, Glass and Pottery Review.

Our New York Salesroom, 68-70 West Broadway.

INTERIOR OF THE J. B. OWENS POTTERY CO.'S NEW YORK SHOWROOM.

8

J. B. Owens

John Bartle Owens II - better known as J. B. Owens - was born on a farm near Roseville, Ohio on December 21st, 1859. He was the seventh child of the eight children born to George Washington Owens I and Mary Ann Rockhold Owens, attended school until the age of 16, and afterwards tried his hand at clerking in stores, working for a sewing machine company and selling insurance. During this time he invested, against the advice of his friends, $20.00 in a watermelon patch and sold it two weeks later at a profit of $50.00. Thus began his life as a businessman. At the age of 19, he became a traveling stoneware salesman for the G. W. Brown Company at a salary of $30.00 per month, eventually becoming their highest paid salesman.

At the age of 25, Owens, having paid $300 for a small dilapidated Roseville, Ohio Pottery with only one wheel and one kiln, established a pottery operation there on January 11, 1885. Though inexperienced in pottery making, he had enough confidence in himself and his selling abilities to hire a potter to make a few kilns of ware while he went on the road to sell it. Within two weeks, he had sold the first kiln of pottery, and, after a few selling trips, had enough money to expand. His new plant and business soon became the largest in Roseville. Owens possessed the instincts of a manufacturer. The exact cost of his products were always known and he was able to accurately gauge the taste of the buying public, changing the styles and kinds of his pottery as necessary to meet that taste. In addition, he acquired a deep practical knowledge of clays, and added to it by unceasing experiments. What he lacked, however, was adequate facilities for shipping the pottery out of Roseville.

The Zanesville Board of Trade in 1891, having learned of Owens shipping problems, offered him $1,500.00, and a free site for building a new plant if he would move his business to Zanesville. After negotiating the cash amount to $3,500.00, Owens agreed. The first stone of his new building was laid on September 2nd of that year, and the first kiln of pottery in the new building was burned on December 15th. He also purchased a 100 acre farm next to the building site and converted it into a subdivision. Business grew rapidly, and by 1894, the adding of new additions had increased the size of the building from the original 55,000 square feet to 175,000 square feet. In 1895 Owens went from producing cheaper grades of ware to a better quality of glazed and ornamental items, and in 1896 produced the Utopian line, his first line of art pottery. This was to be followed over a period of years by many more new lines of art pottery.

With business booming and a banner year expected, Owens had a serious setback when his factory caught fire on Sunday, March 2, 1902. It was discovered by men on duty at the plant at 9:45 a.m., and within three hours the plant was in ruins. (The fire was reported on in detail in the Monday, March 3, 1902 editions of the *Zanesville Evening Signal* and the *Zanesville Daily Courier*.) An interesting excerpt from a *Zanesville Daily Courier* full page article about the March 2 fire is, *"At the Owens pottery the crowd soon began to sack the building, and despite the efforts of the police succeeded in carrying away hundreds of dollars worth of valuable ware. As a large number of persons in the employ of the company were engaged in carrying ware from the burning buildings it was next to impossible for the police to detect those persons who were there by their own bidding and for their own gain."* It was the costliest fire in Zanesville's history to that date, with the factory suffering a $250,000 loss, only $143,000 of which was covered by insurance. The factory, having been rebuilt as fast as possible, was back in operation by August, but, in the meantime, even with his backstock of pottery destroyed, Owens secured temporary quarters and promised to have new stock ready by March 20th. It is also interesting to note that, even as he watched the fire burning, Owens was across the street at the plant of the Ohio Pottery Company making arrangements to lease a portion of their plant. Owens, as indicated by the following article from the June, 1902 issue of *Brick*, was intent on keeping his customers happy. *"The plant of the J. B. Owens Pottery Co., which was recently destroyed by fire at Zanesville, O., is being rebuilt as fast as possible. The entire plant was destroyed. Only the kilns were left standing, and all the buildings and machinery will be new throughout. The new plant will be up-to-date in every particular. The concern is, at this writing, making all of its ware at the plant of the Ohio Pottery Co., which is located just across the street. The ware is then carried across the street and fired in the company's own kilns and is then taken back to the other works to be packed. This method of handling probably cuts all of the profit out of the output, but the company is trying to keep its own trade at least partially supplied."*

After the fire, Owens received offers from several cities trying to lure him to their vicinity to build his new factory. Buffalo, New York was one and East Liverpool, Ohio was another. Another city, of which Owens would not disclose the identity, offered him $60,000, five acres of land for a building site and five acres around the buildings. Owens seemed to indicate he would consider cities which offered him $100,000. At one time it seemed certain he would move to East Liverpool, but, in the end, he decided to remain in Zanesville. Whether or not the city of Zanesville offered him any incentive is unknown.

Owens purchased the Corona Pottery in Corona, Long Island, New York in July, 1902, and soon had the production of the Corona line under way. Although the trade magazines stated that Owens purchased "The" Corona Pottery, it would have likely been more correct to say he purchased "a" Corona Pottery. Research indicates the pottery plant purchased by Owens was, most probably, the American Art-Ceramic Company which had been incorporated on December 13, 1901. Their products, as described in Evans' *"Art Pottery of the United States"*, sound remarkably like Owens' Corona line. The same research eliminated the Corona Pottery, owned by Anton Benkert, and the Volkmer Pottery, owned by Charles Volkmer, as possibilities of the plant purchased by Owens.

In October 1905, Owens, under the name of the Zanesville Tile Company, added tile to the products he made, and a tile plant in close proximity to the pottery plant was expected to be completed in 1906. Owens stated he did not intend to abandon any part of the art ware business, but an article in the January 11, 1906, edition of the *Crockery and Glass Journal* indicates his determination to considerably elevate the standard of his products, that only high grade goods would be made by the company thereafter, and many of the former lines were to be dropped. Presumably, this meant the mass-produced lines of jardinieres, pedestals, cuspidors, vases, etc., and possibly some of the art pottery lines.

Contrary to most written accounts, Owens did not go into bankruptcy or receivership in 1907, nor did he quit making pottery. In June (?) of 1907, Owens sold the Zanesville Tile Company to a group of Columbus, Ohio, capitalists for approximately $45,000, most of it cash. Although it is not entirely clear, it seems that both the pottery and the tile company were included in the transaction. On November 11, 1907, the tile company, due to internal dissension, and the illness of Harry L. Mooar, the company general manager, requested and received receivership status. Owens, in late 1908, persuant to a court order, took charge of the affairs of the tile company, and in early 1909, an involuntary petition of bankruptcy was filed against the company. Accordingly, Owens purchased the personal property of the company, valued at $30,000, for $5,500, and the plant was sold at auction in September, 1909, for $68,600 to William M. Shinnick, treasurer and general manager of the Mosaic Tile Company. Owens was the secondary bidder. Since Owens held about 90% of the claims against the tile company, it seems that not only did he not go into receivership, but probably made a substantial profit overall. Shinnick, on August 24, 1911, sold the plant to the Brush Pottery Company with the restriction that no floor, wall, or fireplace tile was to be manufactured, sold or stored therein. George Brush, in November of the same year, sold it to the J. W. McCoy Company.

According to records at the office of the Ohio Secretary of State, the J. B. Owens Pottery Company was dissolved on April 19th, 1907. However, this was undoubtedly done to facilitate the sale of the pottery and tile company shortly thereafer. Owens had an extensive display at the Jamestown Ter-Centennial Exposition in Norfolk, Virginia from April 26th to November 30th, 1907. *The Glass and Pottery World* magazine of May, 1908, stated *"At the Owens pottery nothing but the very best ware is now produced. "*, and the same magazine for June, 1908, stated *"Weller, Roseville and Owens have each brought out some exceptionally meritorious lines this year. "* While these positively confirm Owens was still making pottery, exactly where he made the pottery is a mystery. No information concerning the operation and demise of Owens' Corona, New York pottery plant has been uncovered and this offers one possibilty. In 1906 and 1907, the trade magazines repeatedly stated that Owens was going to build a new plant in New York City, Jersey City, New Jersey, or elsewhere. An example is *Glass and Pottery World* for November, 1907, which stated *"Rumor persistently credits Mr. Owens as about to build a handsome plant at or near Passaic, N. J. This is not yet a fixed fact, although the erecting of a large model pottery somewhere near New York or Philadelphia is a foregone conclusion. "* Whether or not a new plant was built in the east is unknown, but it is known that in 1905, Owens had the J. B. Owens Ceramic Art Studio at 74 Murray Street in New York City. It is also possible Owens leased space from the Zanesville Tile Company or another pottery in Zanesville.

Within hours after the sale of the Zanesville Tile Company plant at auction in September, 1909, Owens authorized the construction of a new plant in Zanesville for the purpose of manufacturing tile. According to the trade magazines, it was to be incorporated as the Zanesville Floor and Wall Tile Company, but, if so, it only held that name for a short time as the 1910 Zanesville City Directory listed it as the J. B. Owens Floor and Wall Tile Company. Among the listing of the products made were art vases, jardinieres, etc., accordingly confirming Owens was still making art pottery in 1910. It is uncertain what new lines, if any, Owens made after 1907, but pieces of pottery have been found which are different from any of the known lines. It is also uncertain when Owens quit making pottery, but it is not likely that he did so for more than a year or two after 1910.

In 1914, Owens built an additional plant in Metuchen, New Jersey, and, about that time, the name of the company was changed to the Empire Floor and Wall Tile Company. In 1917, he developed the J. B.

Owens Continuous Tunnel Kiln, one of his most profitable enterprises, and, by 1919, the J. B. Owens Tile and China Company, which produced a line of vitrified hotel china, was in operation. The Empire Floor and Wall Tile Company was reorganized and incorporated in Ohio in 1923. Subsequently it was expanded several times, and into other states, by mergers and the building of new facilities.

On March 1, 1928, the Empire plant in Zanesville was destroyed by fire. Rebuilding began immediately, and, by July of the same year, floor and wall tile were again being manufactured. The Metuchen, New Jersey plant took care of the orders during the down period. Again, contrary to written accounts that the plant never began operations after rebuilding, it was open, business was flourishing, and the future looked bright until the stock market crash of 1929. The losses caused by the fire, and the business depression of the stock market crash, weakened the financial stability of the company, and it went into receivership sometime thereafter. Owens then moved to Florida and died there in 1934 at the age of 75.

As shown in the following old trade magazine excerpt, Owens, in the treatment of his employees, was far ahead of his time. Once he was back in business after the 1902 fire, everyone of the artists who worked for him before the fire returned to work for him again.

CHINA, GLASS AND POTTERY REVIEW - December 1901 - *Notes on Art Potteries. "One is strongly reminded of "guilds", which used to be the feature of the manufacturer in medieval days, in a few instances where modern manufacturers have made their works not only places where men could find employment, but where they could enjoy a certain degree of social intercourse. When an artisan is treated in a fraternal spirit he shows his appreciation by the increased excellence of his work. To cite an instance which may be found in the pottery industry, we would mention the J. B. Owens Pottery Co., of Zanesville, Ohio. In this pottery the proprietors have expended considerable money in fitting up a very commodious dining-room, where employees may have hot meals served at the noon hour at a very nominal cost. They have, in connection with this, a reading-room, and the employees all have lockers where they can place their hats and coats and feel that they are under lock and key. The factory, a cut of which is shown in this issue, is one of the most complete in the country. A monthly journal is published by the concern and sent to all customers and people interested in the trade. The plant necessary to bring out this journal is maintained on the place, and this is another instance of the progressiveness of the pottery. We do not know of another instance where a complete printing plant has been installed in such a works. With such surroundings, it is not surprising, that the product of the Owens Pottery is fast achieving world-wide celebrity. Every article that is sent out is carefully inspected and has to be perfect."*

Owens had many varied business interests which it is not possible or necessary to detail herein. The following excerpt from J. Hope Sutor's *"Past and Present of the City of Zanesville, etc.",* which was published in 1905, when Owens was about 45 years old, indicates what the people of Zanesville thought about him.

"Mr. Owens had been a resident of Zanesville but a brief period when he was elected on the democratic ticket to the office of city councilman. He was at once made chairman of the two most important committees of the council, those on finance and law, and he acted as alderman for three terms, when he declined further election. Largely owing to his efforts various streets were paved and improved, sidewalks were laid and there was a great reduction in the cost of lighting and other expenses of the city. He was very successful in all that he did in behalf of Zanesville and his efforts proved of great benefit to the city. Mr. Owens was also president of the Board of Trade and served as director of the Citizens' League, thus being connected with two institutions whose value is well known. He is a stockholder in two of the leading national banks of Zanesville and he is a director in the old Citizens' National Bank. Fraternally he is connected with the Odd Fellows Lodge, with David Encampment and with the Benevolent and Protective Order of Elks.

He takes great pleasure in the society of his friends. He is always courteous, kindly and affable, and those who know him personally have for him warm regard. A man of great natural ability, his success in business, from the beginning of his residence in Zanesville, was uniform and rapid. As has been truly remarked, after all that may be done for a man in the way of giving him early opportunities for obtaining the requirements which are sought in the schools and in books, he must essentially formulate, determine and give shape to his own character, and this is what Mr. Owens has done. He has persevered in the pursuit of a persistent purpose and gained the most satisfactory reward. His life is exemplary in all respects and he has ever supported those interests which are calculated to uplift and benefit humanity, while his own high moral worth is deserving of the highest commendation."

Owens' Pottery

For simplification in writing this book, Owens' Pottery has been divided into two categories, namely: Majolica Finish and Art Pottery.

The meaning of these terms as used here are intentionally broad, and while they may not strictly adhere to the pottery industry definition of these terms, they serve well to separate the two basic kinds of pottery made by Owens.

MAJOLICA FINISH includes the lower grades of glazed pottery that Owens made from 1895 to 1905. Owens' first products in 1885 were common unglazed flower pots, but he quickly added fancy flower pots, lawn vases, cuspidors, umbrella stands, etc., and in 1895 he began producing a better quality of

Salesman's Business Card (Actual Size)

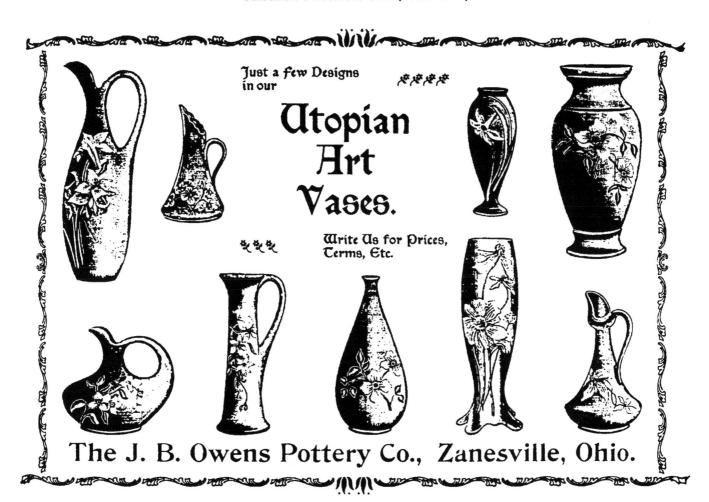

Owens Advertisement

glazed and ornamental stoneware. Some of the fancier glazed (majolica finish) stoneware was produced with line names such as Clifton, Delruba, Empress, Goldenrod, Pompeiian, Rockingham, Royal Worcester, etc. Although he made quantities of majolica finish pottery, including some spectacular jardinieres and pedestals, the primary focus of attention by collectors has been on his art pottery.

ART POTTERY includes the higher grade pottery which Owens produced, starting with the Utopian line, from 1896 until he quit making pottery. This includes slip decorated pieces, incised pieces, squeeze bag decorated pieces, animal statues, pieces with special finishes, etc., and some later made pieces which begin to approach in design and appearance the mass-produced commercial lines made by Weller and Roseville. Had Owens continued making pottery, he would have undoubtedly been involved in making a similar type of commercial pottery. The main focus of this book is on the art pottery.

Identification of Owens' Art Pottery

Marked pieces of Owens' pottery are, of course, easy to identify, but it is not always easy to identify unmarked ones.

Saying that one can identify a piece of Utopian from a piece of Louwelsa or Rozane by the difference in the color of the browns is not a reliable identification. While some tints may be suggestive of Owens, a slight difference in firing temperatures, etc. at any pottery can produce variations in coloring, and make any positive identification on the basis of color shading alone extremely questionable.

Shapes are a much better means of identification. Some pieces, although they may not otherwise be marked, have a shape number on the bottom. So that these pieces, should they be Owens, may be more easily identified, shape numbers, when known, have been included in the pottery descriptions listed in this book. If the numbers and shape match, it is a piece of Owens.

Occasionally, pieces with no numbers can be identified by comparing them to the shapes in the book, or by comparing them to identically shaped marked pieces. Some shapes are unique to Owens and thus may be identified as Owens. Other shapes, however, are so common, nearly identical to those made by Weller, Roseville, etc., that positive identification of these pieces by shape alone is impossible. In comparing shapes, be sure that all curvatures and other features are exactly the same. Due to the shrinkage and settling of the clay, heights may vary slightly in small pieces, and by as much as ½" or more in very large pieces.

Pieces marked with only a line name can usually be identified. See the Line Name Markings page and the list of line names elsewhere in this book. In the line names list are some names which are unique to Owens. Examples are Cyrano, Feroza, Gun Metal, Opalesce, Red Flame, etc. Pieces with line names which were only used by Owens are, of course, Owens.

Owens also produced some lines with unique decorations which can be unmistakenly identified, even if otherwise unmarked. For example, the Mission line and the Cyrano line (with its *raised off the surface* squeeze bag decorations) were made solely by Owens. By familiarizing one's self with these unique decorations, unmarked pieces of Owens can often be identified.

Shapes and Shape Numbers

Many (not all) pieces of Owens Pottery have a shape number consisting of two to four digits on the bottom. The shapes are sequentially numbered, and the range of numbers found so far are from #01 to #1326. Accordingly, it seems Owens must have made more than 1,000 different shapes of art pottery. In addition, he made numerous shapes (named or numbered separately) of majolica finish pottery. The art pottery shapes were used for many of the different lines of art pottery, so it is possible to find the same shape in a number of different lines.

Factory made lamp bases of standard shapes often have an S or AS prefix added to the shape number, thus becoming, for example: S1, or AS9. Some lines, like Aborigine, had its own set of two digit shape numbers, and one of the later Lotus lines had an X prefix in front of the standard shape number, the shape having been altered by adding a molded design. Other variations, not yet apparent, are probabilities.

Other Numbers and Letters

Other numbers, letters, Roman Numerals, etc. may be found on the bottoms of some Owens pieces. Some may be marks used on experimental pieces or process marks relating to records kept at the factory, however, the meaning of these marks are largely unknown. In some cases, the artist's initials are also found on the bottom.

Distribution

An article on page # 12 of the June 11, 1904 issue of *China, Glass and Lamps* states *"Manager Brush, of the J. B. Owens Pottery Co., Zanesville, O., says trade south is good and that north, east and west it is just a little below normal. This company have (has) 39 salesmen on the road, and they are able to thoroughly cover every section quickly where there is any trade movement. Each department of their plant is in full operation."* An excerpt from another article in the May, 1905 issue of *Glass and Pottery World* reads as follows: *"Forty-three men, mostly on salary are covering the country for this enterprising concern and they are well backed up. Mr. Brush is a past master in the art of "speeding the sales force.""*

In addition to the traveling salesmen, sales outlets for Owens' pottery were established in some larger U.S. cities. Following are the addresses where some of these sales outlets were located. The years listed are the times (taken from old advertisements) when they were known to be there, and the names listed are known managers or employees at these outlets. It is likely they were there for additional years other than those listed, and, perhaps, at other addresses.

Since the New York City outlet was often listed (and sometimes pictured) in Owens' advertisements, it was, undoubtedly, the largest and best of the outlets. Articles in old trade magazines indicate that Owens visited the New York City outlet store several times a year.

Although no mention of them has yet been found, it is possible, if not probable, Owens had outlet stores in other large U. S. cities.

CITY	YEAR(S)	LOCATION	EMPLOYEES
Baltimore	1905-06	7 Clay Street, Ripple Building	L. C. Grove
Boston	1898	185 Franklin Avenue	C.H. Osmon & W.S. McPhail
	1903	64 Federal Street	
	1905	146 Franklin Street	
Chicago	1901	406 Garden Building	I. N. Frank
	1904-05	514 Hartford Building	W. S. Redfield
	1906	186 to 188 Fifth Avenue - 4th Floor	Redfield & D.W. Crawford

New York City		12 Murray Street	
	1896	15 Park Place	W. H. Dunn
	1896-1905	68 and 70 West Broadway	W. H. Dunn
	1906	66 West Broadway	Geo.L. Padgett & A. W. Berg
	1906	66 West Broadway	John H. Ling
	1906-1907	147 West 23rd	This showroom was originally

established for showing tile only, but by 1907 was also displaying pottery.

Philadelphia	1899	1113 Market Street - Room 20	Ed M. Jessup
	1900	1111 Market Street	Ed M. Jessup
	1903-05	1035 Market Street	

Pittsburgh	1905-06	420 Bissell Block

Portland, Oregon	1905	46-48 Front Street

Owens gave special attention to the foreign market with known shipments going to Argentina, Australia, Brazil, Canada, Chile, England, France, Germany, New Zealand, and the West Indies.

Advertising and Trade Magazine Information

Owens advertised, or was written about, in the *Crockery and Glass Journal; American Pottery Glassette; Glass and Pottery World; China, Glass and Pottery Review; China, Glass and Lamps*, and other turn of the century trade magazines. If it were not for these magazines, much of the information included in this book would not be available.

Catalogs and Literature

Prior to 1896, Owens' trade advertising mostly contained *"Write us for prices and illustrations," "Send for our illustrated sheets,"* and other similar listings, but the December 30, 1896 issue of *China, Glass and Lamps* states *"the company will be ready to mail their new catalogue to the trade in a few weeks"*, and a catalog of Palm Jars, Pedestals, and Jardinieres was listed as being available in 1899. Then in 1901, *"Send for our Monthly Journal"* was added. In 1903, *"Send for catalog"* appeared, and later there were 1904, 1905, and 1906 catalogs offered.

The 1904 catalog contained: *"17 Lines of Jardinieres, 15 Lines of Pots and Pedestals, 12 Lines of Umbrella Stands, 8 Lines of Cuspidors, 5 Lines of Pitchers, Ducks, Baskets, Money Banks, Crysanthemum Holders, Stewers, Nappies, Butter Jars, Fire Clay Gas Logs, Mission Vases and Jardinieres, Utopian Vases, Henry Deux Line, Venetian Art Line, Corona Animals, and a host of new novelties"*.

The 1905 forty page 11" x 15" catalog was advertised as showing the: *"Strongest line of Fancy and Staple pottery ever shown by one factory in America including 36 distinct lines of Jardinieres, 23 lines of Pots and Pedestals, 16 new Fern Dishes, Exclusive line Wall Ornaments, Exclusive line Rustic Ware, 20 Umbrella Stands, Best line of Cuspidors, Pitchers, Money Banks, Tobacco Boxes, etc., we have ever shown, Nappies, Bowls, Spice Jars, Butter Jars, Stews, Salt Jars, Toilet Sets and Specialties, Art Vases, Pottery Animals, Gas Logs."*

Ads for the 1906 catalog simply stated *"Send for mammoth catalog."* Since the 1896 listing stated "new" catalog, there may have been "old" catalogs before that time. In any case, it seems safe to assume that catalogs were issued from 1896 to 1906, and, perhaps, before, and after.

Since Owens produced, apparently beginning in 1901, a 16 page monthly trade journal, *"The Owens Monthly"*, with a circulation of 10,000 copies here in the United States and abroad, it is likely a sizable number of these catalogs were also printed. It is unknown if any copies of the catalogs and monthly bulletins still exist. Extensive efforts were made to locate catalogs and monthly bulletins in libraries, museums and other institutions throughout the United States, but none were ever found.

Expositions and Exhibits

Owens exhibited at the Lewis and Clark Centennial Exposition in Portland, Oregon in 1905, and won four gold medals and a grand prize. He also exhibited at the Jamestown Ter-Centennial Exposition in Norfolk, Virginia in 1907, and may possibly have exhibited in one or more of the other 5 U.S. and International Expositions held between 1897 and 1904.

In January of 1899 (and perhaps before), Owens had a display at the Pittsburgh Glass Exhibit which was held yearly in January at the Monongahela House in Pittsburgh. The exhibit was comprised of the displays set up by 30 to 40 glass manufacturers and 2 to 3 pottery manufacturers. Merchandise buyers from all over the United States and Canada came to the exhibit to order products for resale. Owens seemed to do well at the exhibit and displayed there for years. A comment on Owens' January, 1905, display at the exhibit from the *Crockery and Glass Journal* of February 2, 1905 is as follows: *"The J. B. Owens Pottery*

Co.'s display showed more than the usual attractions at this Exhibition, and Mr. Israel's rooms were a popular resort for every buying visitor. The quaint sign at the door - an owl with brilliant electric eyes - escaped no one's attention. It was the largest display of quaint, original fetching pottery creations ever shown by a single plant."

Potters, Chemists and Others at Owens

The following has been compiled from old trade magazines, newspaper articles, and books on pottery. A possibility of some errors exist as these sources do not always present, especially on dates, the exact same information.

BRUSH, GEORGE S. Became director of the printing office in 1901 and sales manager in 1905. A fully equipped printing office, under his direction, was maintained to produce advertising material as well as The Owens Monthly, a widely distributed trade journal. He later established the Brush Pottery Company in 1906.

FERRELL, FRANK L. D. Joined Owens in 1907.

GEIJSBEEK (GEYSBECK), SAMUEL. Joined Owens in January of 1896 as manager of the art department and was later promoted to general superintendent of the company. Geijsbeek was born in Holland in 1870, studied chemistry and ceramics in Germany, and, after coming to the United States, completed a two year ceramics course at Ohio State University. He resigned from Owens in June of 1897. Geijsbeek is credited with creating the Utopian line.

HERB, HUGO. A wax work expert from Berlin, Germany, who became a modeler for Owens in 1906.

HEROLD, JOHN J. A designer and artist who later started the Herold China Company which became the Coors China Company.

HOWARTH, GUIDO. An artist of international fame from Budapest, Hungary. Took charge of Owens' decorating department in 1906.

LAGENBECK, KARL. Was hired in late 1891 or early 1892 as head chemist to test clays and glazes. Lagenbeck originally resided in Cincinnati, Ohio, and became the first ceramic chemist in America. In 1886 he founded the Avon Pottery Co., which he operated for one and one half years. Along with Herman C. Mueller in 1894, he organized the Mosaic Tile Co. of Zanesville, Ohio.

LESSELL, JOHN. Became foreman at Owens in 1905.

LONG, WILLIAM A. Left Weller in 1899 and became art director for Owens. Owned the Lonhuda Pottery before he went to Weller.

OWENS, GEORGE NEWTON. Owens' nephew. An excellent artist and glaze developer who was at one time manager of Owens' art department.

OWENS, HERBERT BARTLE. Owens' nephew. Was at one time general manager of the pottery and later the tile plant.

OWENS, MARY MANTONYA. Owens' niece who also worked as one of his artists.

OWENS, STEPHEN WILLIAM III. Owens' brother. Had a small pottery of his own in Crooksville about 1889, and became superintendent of Owens' Pottery about 1891.

RADFORD, ALBERT. Worked at Owens as superintendent and modeler from 1901 to 1903. Became general manager of the A. Radford Pottery Company in Clarksburg, West Virginia in 1904.

Owens Advertisement

22

Years Lines Were Introduced

It is said that Owens duplicated every line made by Weller and Roseville, and created new lines of his own. Below are the dates on which Owens' known lines were introduced. The line names marked with an * are names which have been created to identify lines of which the original Owens names are unknown. Hopefully some of these will be correctly identified after additional research.

(?)   Creamware*
      Korina
      Lightweight*
      Silver Overlay Utopian

1895 - Majolica Finish

1896 - Utopian

1898 - Cyrano
       Onyx
       Oriental

1899 - American Awaja Ware

1900 - Henri Deux
       Poster

1901 - Art Nouveau
       Feroza

1902 - Corona
       Matt Utopian

1903 - Corona Animals
       Jasper Art
       Metal Deposit
       Mission
       Multi-Color Blends
       Rainbow Bronze
       Transfer*
       Venetian

1904 - Rustic

1905 - Alpine
       Art Vellum
       Delft
       Gun Metal
       Jeweled*
       Matt Green
       Opalesce
       Opalesce Inlaid
       Opalesce Utopian
       Persian
       Red Flame
       Tile

1906 - Brushmodel Lotus
       Corona Green
       Embossed Lotus*
       Lotus
       Monochrome Art
       Parchment Lotus
       Semi-Glazed Etched
       Sunburst
       Sylvan Green

1907 - Aborigine
       Aqua Verdi
       Old Copper
       Soudaneze

Company Marks On Owens Pottery

EMBOSSED:

Mark # 1: To date, only majolica finish pottery has been found with embossed (raised) marks. Pre-1905 and mostly Pre-1900.

INCISED:

Mark # 2: Numerous examples of incised JBO monogram type marks have been found. They were used on both majolica finish and art pottery. Although used on some majolica finish pottery before 1896, the period of most usage was 1896 to 1906. Here are a few examples:

INCISED:

Occasionally, fully written J. B. Owens incised marks will be found. They were used on both majolica finish and art pottery. Although used on some majolica finish pottery before 1896, the period of most usage was 1896 to 1906.

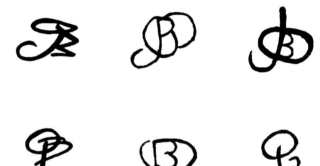

Mark # 3

Mark # 4

IMPRESSED:

See notes on these marks
following the illustrations.

Mark # 7

Mark # 8

**The
J. B. Owens
Pottery Co.**

Mark # 5

Mark # 6

J.B. OWENS

Mark # 9

OWENS

Mark # 10

OWENS

Mark # 11

OWENS

Mark # 12

Owens

Mark # 13

J. B. Owens

Mark # 14

OWENSART

Mark # 15

OWENZART

Mark # 16

Mark # 5:   Seen on pieces of majolica finish pottery.

Mark # 6:   Illustrated in pottery mark guides, but the only place I've ever seen it used is in trade
magazine advertisements starting in 1907.

Marks # 7 and # 15: Introduced in 1905 in Owens' Display at the Lewis and Clark Centennial
Exposition in Portland, Oregon. Mark # 7 is referred to as the "Torch" mark.

Mark # 8:   Used mostly on Lightweight.

Marks # 9 through # 16: Some of these marks were used in both capital and small letters in various
sizes, both larger and smaller.

Mark # 16: This mark has an obvious spelling error, -- Z for S --, but was still used on a number of
pieces of pottery.

PAPER LABELS:

The use of paper labels on pottery was fairly common, and, although none has yet been
found with Owens Pottery Company marks on them, two have been found with Owens Line
Name marks (see Line Name Marks). Accordingly, it is probable paper labels were used,
especially on otherwise unmarked pottery.

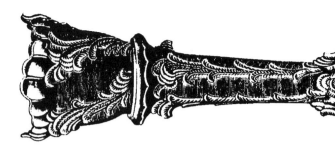

No. 5540.
Jardiniere, blended colors.

A FEW OF OUR NEWEST DESIGNS
IN JARDINIERES AND PEDESTALS

Write for Prices while we have goods in stock.

THE J. B. OWENS POTTERY CO.

ZANESVILLE, OHIO.

Manufacturers of Color Glazed Jardinieres, Umbrella Stands,
Cuspidors, Pitchers, Art Vases, Steins, etc.

NEW YORK OFFICE,
68-70 West Broadway.

PHILADELPHIA OFFICE,
1113 Market Street.

No. 5560.
Dolphin Jardiniere and Pedestal,
in blended colors or decorated.

Advertisement from the June 15, 1900, Issue of *The Illustrated Glass and Pottery World.*

Line Name Markings

These marks were placed on the bottom of the pottery to identify the line to which it belonged, and were taken from actual pieces of pottery. It is expected that other marks will be found. Some of these marks were used in both capital and small letters in various sizes, both larger and smaller. Occasionally Owens, as did other pottery manufacturers, marked the wrong name on a piece. Some, but not all, pieces of Owens' Pottery were marked with line names.

UTOPIAN	**Utopian**	***Utopian***	Utopian
Impressed	Impressed	Impressed	Impressed

			HENRI
ART NOUVEAU	**CYRANO**	**FEROZA**	**DEUX**
Impressed	Impressed	Impressed	Impressed

Henri Deux	**LOTUS**	*Lotus*	*Lotus*
Impressed	Impressed	Incised	Incised

Matt Green	Mission Pottery	**ORIENTAL**	**SOUDANEZE**
Impressed	Painted on Bottom	Impressed	Impressed

SUN BURST	*Sunburst*	VENETIAN	VENETIAN
Impressed	Incised	On paper label	Painted under glaze

POSTER

Impressed

Artists and Their Monograms and Signatures

Some artists also worked for (C) Cambridge, (CA) Camark, (L) Lonhuda, (P) Peters and Reed, (R) Roseville, (RF) Radford, (RK) Rookwood, (W) Weller or (Z) Zane.

Adams, Virginia (R) (W)

Asbury, Lenore (RK)

Beardsley, Estelle

Bell, Edith

Bell, Fanny

Best, Anna Fulton (R) (W)

Bloomer, Cecilia

Bloomer, Lillian

Burgess, Levi J. (W)

Butterworth, John (R) (W)

Chilcote, Charles (R) (W) (Z)

Cook, Daniel (RK)

Davis, Cora

Denny, Walter

Eberlein, Harrie (Harry?)

HE HE

Eberlein, Hattie

HE "HE"

Excel, Cecil

CE CE CE CE

Ferrell, Frank L. D. (P) (R) (W)

Ferrell— F. F.

Fouts, Charles (W)

F F F

Gillie, Mary (W)

M G m.g.

Gray, Charles (W)

G

Gray, Martha E.

M.G. Gray N.G.

Harvey, Delores (W)

D.H.

Haubrich, Albert (W)

A. Haubrich A. H.
1901.

Herb, Hugo (W)

H. H. H H

Herold, John J. (R) (W)

JH JH J.H.

Hook, Roy (R) (W)

RH RH RH

Hoskins, H.

HH

Hutaf, August W.

Larzelere, Harry (R)

Leffler, Claude L. (R) (W)

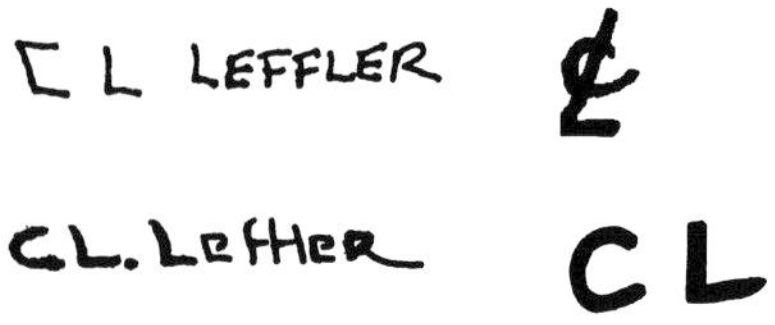

C L LEFFLER

CL. Leffler

Lessell, John B. (CA) (W)

JL

Lewis, A. V. (W)

AL

Long, William A. (L) (W)

McCandless, Cora (W)

McDonald, Carrie

Mallen, Blanche (R)

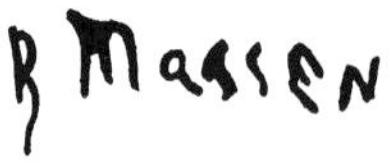

R Mallen

Mitchell, Hattie (R) (W)

H. M.

Niblock, Charles

Unknown

Oshe, Miss

O

Owens, George Newton

Unknown

Owens, Mary Mantonya

Unknown

Pierce, Mary L. (W) (R)

MP M. P.

Pillsbury, Hester (R) (W)

H ; Pillsbury

Pitser, E. B.

EB PITSER

Radford, Albert (RF) (W)

A R

30

Rauchfuss, Marie (RK) (W)

Robinson, Harry (W)

Ross, Hattie M. (W)

Shoemaker, R. Lillian (R) (W)

Smith, Helen (R) (W)

Spaulding, Jesse R. (L) (W)

Steele, Fred (R)

Steele, Ida

Steele, Tot (R) (W)

Stemm, Will H. (W)

Stevens, Mary Fauntleroy

Terry, C. Minnie (W)

Timberlake, Mae (R) (W)

Timberlake, Sara (R) (W)

Upjohn, Charles B. (W)

Williams, Arthur (C) (R)

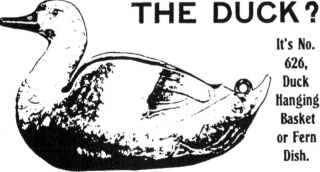

Color Section
With Information on Owens' Pottery Lines

The color photographs in this section vary considerably in quality as many were provided by Owens collectors. It seemed better to use some of these less than perfect photographs than not show the Owens' pottery they picture.

♦ ♦ ♦ ♦ ♦ ♦ ♦ ♦ ♦ ♦ ♦ ♦ ♦ ♦

The line names marked with an * are names which have been created to identify lines of which the original Owens' names are unknown. Hopefully some of these will be correctly identified after additional research.

♦ ♦ ♦ ♦ ♦ ♦ ♦ ♦ ♦ ♦ ♦ ♦ ♦ ♦

Pieces with company marks of a regular style are listed by the Mark Number.

♦ ♦ ♦ ♦ ♦ ♦ ♦ ♦ ♦ ♦ ♦ ♦ ♦ ♦

Even though a piece of pottery may have been marked only with the artist's monogram, the artist's full name has been included in the following color section. If only a monogram is listed, the artist has not yet been identified. If no monogram is given, the piece was either unsigned, or the artist's marking was illegible.

♦ ♦ ♦ ♦ ♦ ♦ ♦ ♦ ♦ ♦ ♦ ♦ ♦ ♦

The last listed and identified lines were made in 1907, but Owens was still solidly in business in 1908, and through 1910, and most likely, made some, if only a few, new lines during this period. Some of these are undoubtedly included in the UNIDENTIFIED AS TO LINE section.

♦ ♦ ♦ ♦ ♦ ♦ ♦ ♦ ♦ ♦ ♦ ♦ ♦ ♦

The LINES WITHOUT PICTURES section lists other known lines for which pictures are not yet available.

♦ ♦ ♦ ♦ ♦ ♦ ♦ ♦ ♦ ♦ ♦ ♦ ♦ ♦

Excerpts, when available, from various old trade magazines have been included under the line name listings. Some excerpts are misleading, datewise, as the best pottery line descriptions were sometimes written a year or two after the pottery was introduced.

♦ ♦ ♦ ♦ ♦ ♦ ♦ ♦ ♦ ♦ ♦ ♦ ♦ ♦

Where pictured in rows, pieces are listed from left to right, and from the top to the bottom row.

♦ ♦ ♦ ♦ ♦ ♦ ♦ ♦ ♦ ♦ ♦ ♦ ♦ ♦

The Owensart trade marks (Marks #7 & #15) were introduced at the Lewis and Clark Centennial Exposition in Portland, Oregon in 1905. Accordingly, any pieces on which they have been used were made in or after 1905.

Aborigine

Introduced in 1907. An Indian-type pottery for which the designs were taken from early Indian pottery at the Smithsonian Institution. Has an earthenware body with the exterior unglazed and the interior glazed in varying colors from honey gold to dark chocolate. Many types of pots, vases, and pitchers, some with handles, were made. The shapes, using two digit numbers, are numbered separately from the other lines, and nearly 100 different shapes may have been made. Have not seen with a line name marked piece.

♦ ♦ ♦ ♦ ♦ ♦ ♦ ♦ ♦ ♦ ♦ ♦ ♦ ♦ ♦

GLASS AND POTTERY WORLD - April 1907 - *"The new Indian assortments, termed the Aborigine line, was fashioned accurately after the artist had carefully examined all of the government exhibits at the Smithsonian Institute at Washington. In coloring and fidelity to shapes it has set a new standard to excellence and also produced at a price most interesting to dealers."*

OPPOSITE PAGE

First Row
1. 2" Bowl. Incised JBO. Shape # 51.
2. 4" Jar. Incised JBO. Shape # 26.
3. 2 5/8" Bowl. Unmarked.

Second Row
4. 5 1/8" Handled Jug. Incised JBO. Shape # 31.
5. 4 3/4" Vase. Unmarked.
6. 3 3/4" Handled Jug. Incised JBO and Mark # 10.

Third Row
7. 5¼" Vase. Incised JBO.
8. 3½" x 11" Bowl. Incised JBO and Mark # 10.
9. 6" Vase. Incised JBO and Mark # 10.

Fourth Row
10. 6 7/8" Vase. Mark # 10.
11. 6 1/8" Bowl. Mark # 10.
12. 7 3/4" Pitcher. Incised JBO.   13.   8 3/4" by 11" Diameter Vase. Incised JBO.

Alpine

Introduced in 1905. Has a freehand overglaze slip decoration in a matt finish, and a soft shaded background in blue, green, and brown colors. Chiefly depicts flowers and fruits, but the tobacco humidors picture cigars, corncob pipes, pouches of tobacco, and matches. Many pieces, but not all, have a white top like a snow-capped mountain. Sometimes marked with the line name.

◆ ◆ ◆ ◆ ◆ ◆ ◆ ◆ ◆ ◆ ◆ ◆ ◆ ◆

CROCKERY AND GLASS JOURNAL - January 19, 1905 - Page # 32. *"Other incomers meriting special reference are the Alpine vases, a line that embodies thirty-six distinct pieces. The grounds are in shaded blues, greens and browns, surmounted by hand-painted flowers similarly colored. The effects produced by the light, delicate tones in this line are especially artistic."*

BELOW

14.   12¼" Vase. Mark #13. "TS" for Tot Steele. Shape # 1122.

15.   8" Vase. Unmarked. Shape #1127. (Photo is actual color)

OPPOSITE PAGE

16.   17 5/8" Vase. Mark # 13. Shape # 1125.

17.   5 7/8" Humidor. Mark #13.

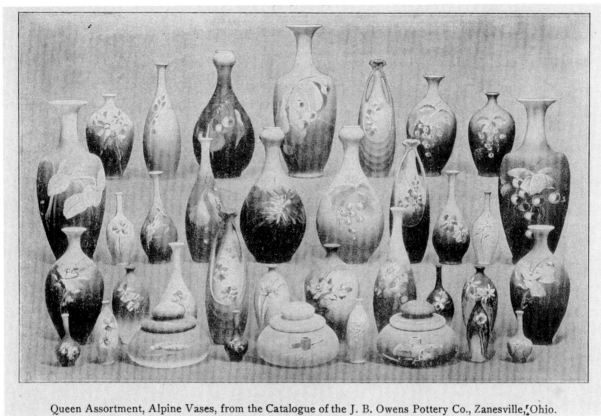

Queen Assortment, Alpine Vases, from the Catalogue of the J. B. Owens Pottery Co., Zanesville, Ohio.

Picture of Alpine Vases from a 1905 issue of China, Glass and Pottery Review.

Aqua Verdi

Introduced in 1907. Matt finished, unevenly surfaced, variegated light to dark green pottery, sometimes with embossed figures. A piece of Aqua Verdi, as illustrated in the October, 1907, issue of *Glass and Pottery World*, is shown here, along with a color picture of an Aqua Verdi piece.

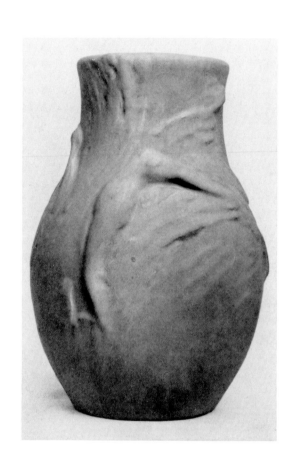

BELOW

18.   3 7/8" Three Handled Vase. Mark # 10. Shape # 234.

ABOVE: An illustration of an Aqua Verdi Vase from the October, 1907, issue of *Glass and Pottery World.*

Art Nouveau

Introduced in 1901. Has a high-gloss glaze with an under glaze decoration of colored swirls on a green to dark brown background. Some pieces have silhouette figures on them. Sometimes marked with the line name.

♦ ♦ ♦ ♦ ♦ ♦ ♦ ♦ ♦ ♦ ♦ ♦ ♦ ♦

CHINA, GLASS & LAMPS - March 8, 1902 - Page # 11 - *"Seven or eight distinct lines of art pottery are manufactured. These include the Utopian, Feroza, Henri Deux, Cyrano, Postier (Poster), Art Nouveau and Korina lines. These lines of art pottery have been introduced and perfected after years of experiment and toil."*

BELOW

19. 7½" Jardiniere. Impressed "J. B. Owens" and "Art Nouveau". Shape # 1005.

20. 6" Jardiniere. Unmarked. Shape # 1005.

21. 5¼" Jardiniere. Impressed "Art Nouveau" only. Shape # 1005.

22. 6 7/8" Vase. Unmarked.

Art Vellum

Introduced in 1905. - Has a soft, smooth, satiny, vellum finish of great delicacy. The pieces are of Utopian coloring and are painted with florals and portraits. Have not seen a line name marked piece.

CROCKERY AND GLASS JOURNAL - August 31, 1905 - Page # 16 - *THE NEW YORK TRADE* - *"One of the J. B. Owens Pottery Co.'s spacious show windows is occupied just now by an exhibit of vases, jardinieres and tankards in the most recent of this factory's color innovations. Brown in the predominant tone employed for the groundwork, but it passes from a deep, rich hue to a tint that is almost yellow. On this are hand-painted floral and fruit decorations in lighter but thoroughly compatible shades. The coloring, however, is but a small part of the ware's virtue. Its matt surface not only looks but feels like velvet. No better specimen of potting has ever emanated from the concern's plant."*

BELOW

23. 5 3/4" Vase. Mark # 13. Shape # 112.
24. 6¼" Jardiniere. Unmarked.
25. 6" Vase with Horse Portrait. Marked Owens. Shape # 1114.
26. 17 3/8" Vase with Indian Portrait. Mark # 14. Titled "Sego Shoshone". "A. F. Best". Shape # 1052.

Corona

Introduced in 1902. This line consists of bronze colored pottery pieces in the shape of statues or vases with figures attached. A 1902 edition of China, Glass and Lamps states "One in particular, a female figure apparently poised upon the crest of a wave, and upholding in her joined hands an electric light, is most graceful and in finish so nearly approximates real bronze that it takes close inspection to note the difference." May be marked Owens or Corona.

CROCKERY AND GLASS JOURNAL - August 28, 1902 - Page # 18 - *"Vases, jardinieres, umbrella stands and the various other shapes in which the Corona ware is modeled are all being favored by heavy orders. The pieces are beautified by artistically modeled dragons, serpents, imitation bronze figures, the latter of which can scarcely be distinguished from genuine bronze."*

CROCKERY AND GLASS JOURNAL - October 2, 1902 - Page # 20 - *"The subjects differ materially from any of the former productions of the concern, and, if such were possible, they are more artistic. One piece represents Satan gazing avariciously at the figure of a woman; another depicts a boy playing a harp for the edification of his sweetheart; still another shows a dragon entwined about the body of the ware."*

RIGHT: Illustration of a piece of Corona Ware from page # 181 of the December 11, 1902, issue of *Crockery and Glass Journal.*

CORONA WARE. ♦ BY THE
J. B. OWENS POTTERY CO.

Corona Animals

Introduced in 1903. Figures of animals with an unglazed earthenware body. These were designed for decorative purposes and could be used indoors, on the porch or on the lawn. They are perfect models of animals, and are finished in natural colors, ranging in size from a Dachshund four and half inches high to a Great Dane forty-three inches high. Foxes, elephants, dogs, bears, bulls, goats, owls, fawns, sheep, cows, rabbits, kittens, squirrels and other animals were made. The animals seen so far have glass eyes. Sometimes marked Owens or Corona.

CHINA, GLASS AND POTTERY REVIEW - March 1905 - *"The other window is at present entirely given up to a display of excellently-modeled animals of many varieties, such as foxes, elephants, various kinds of dogs, bears, cows, rabbits, squirrels and many others. Perched upon a pedestal, overlooking this miniature menagerie, is a great barn owl, the colors of which are as true to nature as the potter's art can make them. An electric battery hidden within this owl causes a continuous blinking of the eyes, which adds materially to the attractiveness of this window."*

BELOW
27. Dog. (Whippet or Greyhound?) Unmarked. Height Unknown.
28. 15" x 13" Rabbit. Marked "Corona". Shape # 8873.

Illustrations of Corona Animals

Creamware*

Introduced in (?). Below is pictured a large Owens' marked high glaze art pottery shaped piece which has a cream color overall with no other decoration. No further information is available.

BELOW

29. 15 1/8" Vase. Mark # 10. Shape # 1126.

Cyrano

Introduced in 1898. Has squeeze bag applied filigree designs in white, tan, blue, buff or brown in the manner of lace. In the case of Cyrano, part of the design is raised off the surface, like a bridge with an open area underneath, while Oriental has all of the design flat on the surface.

CHINA, GLASS & LAMPS - November 9, 1901 - Page # 9 - *"Their "Cyrano" line of vases and art novelties is another product of handsome shapes and filigree overlaid decoration. The body of the ware is dark and the decoration consists of delicate openwork of light material put on in pretty designs, figures and borders and is very ornamental and effective."*

BOTTOM

First Row
30.   6¼" Double Handled Vase. Unmarked. Shape # 357.

Second Row
31.   8¼" Jardiniere. Unmarked.
32.   8 1/8" Jardiniere. Impressed "Cyrano".

Delft

Introduced in 1905. Old Holland bucket, tub and jardiniere shapes ornamented and incised with Dutch scenes in shades of blue.

♦ ♦ ♦ ♦ ♦ ♦ ♦ ♦ ♦ ♦ ♦ ♦ ♦ ♦

CROCKERY AND GLASS JOURNAL - January 19, 1905 - Page # 32 - *THE NEW YORK TRADE* - "In the list of the J. B. Owens Pottery Co.'s ceramic innovations for 1905, now being shown in their entirety at W. H. Dunn's salesroom typical Holland scenes on jardinieres, the incised designs of which are colored in poster-like effects, are among the more noteworthy offerings. The "jars" are in six sizes and fashioned along very graceful lines."

DELFT TUB
Only one of the many exclusive lines.

BELOW

33.   10½" Jardiniere. Unmarked.

Embossed Lotus*

Introduced in 1906. This line is separate from the other Lotus lines in that it has an embossed molded design on a standard shape. The decoration is slip painted atop the embossed areas. See Lotus and Brushmodel Lotus. Often marked Lotus and the shape number has an "X" in front of it.

BELOW

First Row
34. 6" Vase. Mark # 10 and "Lotus". Shape # X218.
35. 8 3/4" Vase. Mark # 10 and "Lotus". Shape # X220.
36. 3" Pitcher. Mark # 10 and "Lotus". Shape # X236.

Second Row
37. 6" Vase. Matt Glaze. Mark # 10 and "Lotus". Shape # X218.
38. 3" Pitcher. Mark # 10 and " Lotus". Shape # X236.

Feroza

Introduced in 1901. A molded ware made in a very dark brownish black color, a deep red color, and, perhaps, other colors. Has a metallic looking finish with slight iridescent effects. Originally made in 22 different shapes, but more shapes may have been added later. Sometimes impressed with the line name.

CHINA, GLASS & LAMPS - November 9, 1901 - Page # 9 - *"A beautiful new product recently brought out by this firm is what is known as the Feroza faience. It is something rare and has required years of experiment to accomplish. It has a decidedly metallic effect in color. The surface of the ware is uneven, while in some pieces rude, embossed outlines of birds, fish, etc., are discernible, giving it a most grotesque appearance. The color is very dark and has a lustre or finish peculiar to bronze metals. This line comprises twenty-two pieces, including vases, tankards, mugs, etc., ranging from four to twenty inches in height. The shapes are ancient and unique."*

BELOW

39. 4 7/8" Red Mug. Marked "Feroza". Shape # 1108.
40. 5½" Double Handled Vase. Marked "Feroza". Shape # 1090.
41. 11¼" Tankard Pitcher. Marked "Feroza". Shape # 1109.

Green Ware

Owens made a number of green colored lines including Aqua Verdi, Corona Green, Matt Green, Rustic and Sylvan Green. Excepting for Rustic, which is easily identified, and some Matt Green pieces which have line name markings, it is difficult to positively identify some pieces. Accordingly, it is possible a green piece could be pictured under the wrong line name even though considerable care has been taken not to let this happen. Green pieces which are not identifiable as belonging to the known lines are shown here. It is probable there are three or more additional green lines which have not yet been identified.

BELOW

First Row

42.   5 7/8" Vase. Mark # 12. Shape # 234 ....(# 42, 43, & 44
43.   2 7/8" Planter. Mark # 12. Shape # 242 ......appear to be of
44.   5 7/8" Mug. Mark # 12. Shape # 46 ....the same line)

Second Row

45.   11" Wall Vase. Marked "Owensart".
46.   8 7/8" Vase. Mark # 10. Shape # 1155. (Corona Green?)

Green Ware - Continued

47. 11¼" Lamp Base. Unmarked. Shape # AS9.
48. 10" Wall Vase. Marked "Owensart". (Aqua Verdi?)
49. 6 7/8" Vase. Mark # 10. Shape # 0225. (Matches a Blue Vase with the Same Shape Number. Perhaps, a Multi-Color Line.)
50. 3" Double Handled Vase. Torch Mark. Shape # 1139. (Corona Green?)

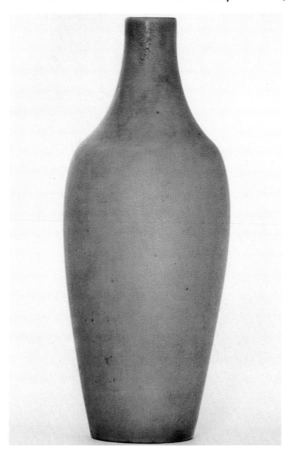

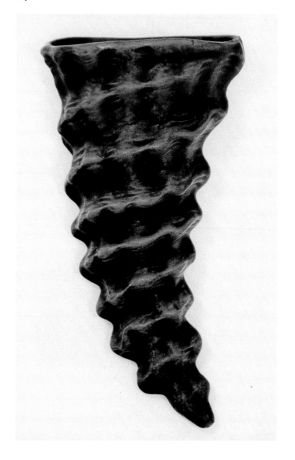

51. 6 3/4" Candlestick Shaped Vase. Mark # 10. Shape # 1157 (Aqua Verdi?)
52. 5¼" Candle Holder. Bottom is impressed "Feb 13 06 - Zanesville Tile Co." (Aqua Verdi?).
53. 11" Vase. Mark # 12. Shape # 328.
54. 9¼" Vase. Mark # 10. Shape # 340.

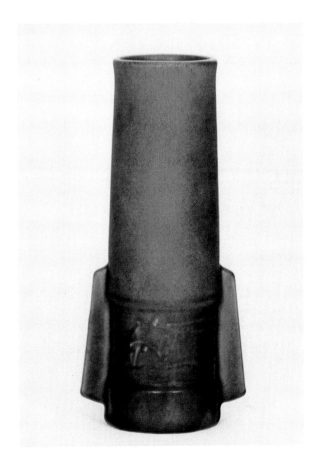

Henri Deux

Introduced in 1900. Features molded pieces with incised designs filled with colored clay. The patterns, often containing women, and which have here-to-fore been described as being Art Nouveau, were actually supposed to be faithful reproductions of the 16th Century originals. The line name, Henri Deux, was derived from the frequent occurrence of that monarch's cypher forming part of the decoration. Besides the usual pottery shapes, ewers, tazzas, salt cellars and plates were also made. Sometimes marked with the line name.

CROCKERY AND GLASS JOURNAL - September 20, 1900 - Page # 21 - *THE NEW YORK TRADE* - "*W. H. Dunn has received samples of the new Henri Deux ware made by the J. B. Owens Pottery Co. This is a distinct departure from their well-known lines, and is a remarkable production. The history of Henri Deux ware is full of interest, dating back to 1537. The "Encyclopedia of Ceramics," published in this journal in 1898, referring to this ware, says: "But fifty-three pieces of the ware remain, and they are valued at $140,000. The ware is a fine white clay, to which a delicate tint is given by a very slight tinge of yellow in the glaze. The patterns, which are very intricate, seem to have been suggested by the highly ornate book covers of the period, of which, doubtless, the library of the chateau furnished many examples. There were first incised or impressed in the clay, and the sunken portions were filled up with different colored clays in yellow, buff or brown. As all these clays had to shrink in exactly the same proportions, the difficulties attending the manufacture can readily be estimated." That the J. B. Owens Co. should produce such excellent imitations is quite a feather in their cap, and there should be a demand for specimen pieces, because of the rarity and beauty of the ware.*"

OPPOSITE PAGE

First Row

55. 8 3/4" Vase. Mark # 10. Shape # 1307.
56. 6 3/4" Vase. Unmarked.
57. 8 3/4" Vase. Unmarked.

Second Row

58. 21" Jardiniere and Pedestal. Impressed "Henri Deux".
59. 22¼" Umbrella Stand. Unmarked.

53

Jeweled*

Introduced in 1905.   An illustration of a vase with embossed round jewels appeared in an Owens' advertisement in the August, 1905 issue of Glass and Pottery World. The Indian vase below also appeared in the same advertisement, and the three medallion like pieces in the head-dress appeared to represent "Jewels". Unfortunately, no line name was given. No further information is available.

<u>BELOW</u>

60.   14" Indian Head Vase. Unmarked.

From Advertisement

Illustrations of Majolica Finish Pottery
from Old Trade Magazines

See Page 70 for "Majolica Finish" Information.

Lightweight*

Introduced in (?). Pottery, mostly of the Utopian type, only of thinner clay. Generally speaking, it is lighter in weight, has more delicate painting, and, if it has a shape number, it is usually in the 700's, or the 800's. The bottom is unglazed and of a white or very light tan clay. Decorations are flowers, fish, etc. Have not seen a line name marked piece.

BELOW

61. 5 7/8" Ewer. Unmarked. Shape # 850.

62. 8 5/8" Handled Vase. Mark # 8. "CE" for Cecil Excel. Shape # 870.

63. 5 3/4" Four Footed Vase. Unmarked. "EB" for Edith Bell. Shape # 821.

64. 10¼" Vase with Fish. Unmarked. Monogram of Harry Larzelere. Shape # 823.

OPPOSITE PAGE

First Row

65. 20" Vase with Cavalier Portrait. Marked. "Anna Fulton Best". Shape # 761.

66. 7 5/8" Stein with Indian Portrait. Marked. Shape # 830.

Second Row

67. 17" Tankard with Woman's Portrait. Marked. "AFB" for Anna Fulton Best. Shape # 819.

68. 10 3/8" Four Footed Vase with Fish. Unmarked. Monogram of Harry Larzelere.

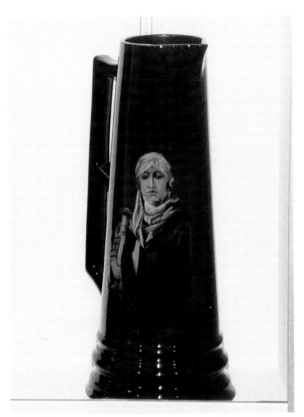

Lightweight - Continued

BELOW

69.   16½" Tankard with Dragon Decoration. Unmarked. Monogram of Unidentified Artist. Shape # 819.

a.   Close-up Photo of Dragon on Piece # 69.

OPPOSITE PAGE

First Row

70.   6 3/4" Ewer. Unmarked. "HR" for Harry Robinson. Shape # 837.
71.   5 7/8" Vase. Unmarked. "CB" for Cecilia Bloomer. Shape # 894.
72.   6 3/8" Vase. Mark # 8. Shape # 804.
73.   6¼" Vase. Unmarked. Shape # 897.

Second Row

74.   6¼" Two Handled Vase. Mark # 8. Shape # 879.
75.   2 3/4" Jug. Marked. Monogram of Harry Larzelere.
76.   6¼" Vase. Incised "JBO". "RH" for Roy Hook. Shape # 865.

Third Row

77.   7 5/8" Stein. Mark # 8. Monogram of Harry Larzelere. Shape # 830.
78.   5½" Jug. Unmarked. "HR" for Harry Robinson. Shape # 791.
79.   7" Vase. Unmarked. Shape # 838.

Lines Without Pictures

American Awaja Ware

Introduced in 1899. This line is listed because of the following old Trade Magazine excerpt. It is unknown if the ware is majolica finish or art pottery, but, most likely, it is majolica finish pottery. No other information is available.

CROCKERY AND GLASS JOURNAL - November 9, 1899 - Page # 17 - *THE NEW YORK TRADE* - "W. H. *Dunn displayed this week in the windows of the J. B. Owens Pottery Co.'s warerooms a fine line of American Awaja ware. It is all right, and is one of the most striking things the pottery ever turned out.*"

◆ ◆ ◆ ◆ ◆ ◆ ◆ ◆ ◆ ◆ ◆ ◆ ◆ ◆ ◆

Brushmodel Lotus

Introduced in 1906. Finished in a matt glaze with a "soft and wax-like luster." See Lotus for more information on the glaze. This line name may belong to the line listed herein as Embossed Lotus*, but no information has been found to confirm this. The decoration on Embossed Lotus* is of simple brush strokes on an embossed molded (modeled?) surface, so it seems to fit well. No further information is available.

◆ ◆ ◆ ◆ ◆ ◆ ◆ ◆ ◆ ◆ ◆ ◆ ◆ ◆ ◆

Corona Green

Introduced in 1906. This line is included because of the following excerpt. No further information is available.

CROCKERY AND GLASS JOURNAL - October 25, 1906 - Page # 27 - *THE NEW YORK TRADE* - "*Several new specimens of J. B. Owens' art ware have been received at J. H. Ling's showroom. The most conspicuous are three pieces clothed in Corona green, which is darker and purer than the former green tones produced by this firm. The shapes are patterned after Egyptian styles.*"

◆ ◆ ◆ ◆ ◆ ◆ ◆ ◆ ◆ ◆ ◆ ◆ ◆ ◆ ◆

Gun Metal

Introduced in 1905. Consists of an unglazed metallic-coated earthenware body with an iridescent finish resembling the rich, dull surface of gun metal into which was often engraved an intricate and delicate design. No further information is available.

GLASS AND POTTERY WORLD - April 1907 - *American Art Pottery - Part III, by Marcus Benjamin.*
"Somewhat resembling the foregoing (Venetian) is the Gun Metal Ware which consists of an earthenware body with an iridescent finish resembling dull gun metal. It is unglazed and the decorations are engraved in intricate design with high lights."

◆ ◆ ◆ ◆ ◆ ◆ ◆ ◆ ◆ ◆ ◆ ◆ ◆ ◆ ◆

Jasper Art (Art Jasper)

Introduced in 1903. Very similar to English Jasperware, and Radford's Jasperware, whereby small previously molded and designed pieces of clay are attached to the main body of a piece. Undoubtedly the work of Albert Radford. Has a blue background with white decorations.

CROCKERY AND GLASS JOURNAL - October 15, 1903 - Page # 21 - *THE NEW YORK TRADE - "There is apparently no limit to the ambitions of the J. B. Owens Pottery Co. in the perfection of art pottery. Scarcely has the trade ceased its commentaries on the "Mission Pottery" and ceramic menagerie than W. H. Dunn opens for observation in the New York salesrooms the Jasper jardinieres and pedestals. A delicate, pleasing shade of blue covers the pieces, which fades very gradually into a white space that permits the application of cameo effects. The flowers used in these decorations emerge apparently from the body of the ware, arising from the blue ground indistinctly at first and becoming more and more discernible only as the floral form assumes its shape. A thickening of color here and there on the flowers gives it a sort of raised effect."*

◆ ◆ ◆ ◆ ◆ ◆ ◆ ◆ ◆ ◆ ◆ ◆ ◆ ◆ ◆

Korina

Introduced in (?). The excerpt below contains the only reference found so far to this line. The pottery in Corona, New York, was not purchased until July of 1902, so it's not likely to be a misspelling of Corona.

CHINA, GLASS & LAMPS - March 8, 1902 - Page # 11 - (After the fire) *J. B. OWENS ART WARE - "Temporary Quarters Have Been Secured And Ware Promised By March 20 - Seven or eight distinct lines of art pottery are manufactured. These include the Utopian, Feroza, Henri Deux, Cyrano, Postier (Poster), Art Nouveau and Korina lines. These lines of art pottery have been introduced and perfected after years of experiment and toil."*

◆ ◆ ◆ ◆ ◆ ◆ ◆ ◆ ◆ ◆ ◆ ◆ ◆ ◆

Multi-Color Blends

Introduced in 1903. Listed in an Owens' advertisement in the October, 1903, issue of China, Glass and Pottery Review. Could be either majorica finish or art pottery. No further information is available.

◆ ◆ ◆ ◆ ◆ ◆ ◆ ◆ ◆ ◆ ◆ ◆ ◆

Old Copper

Introduced in 1907. This line is included because of the following excerpt. Although not positively stated, it seems to indicate a line of "Old Copper" pieces of pottery.

CHINA, GLASS AND LAMPS - October 5, 1907 - Page # 3 - OHIO'S CERAMIC EXHIBIT AT JAMESTOWN EXPOSITION - *"The Owens pottery, also of Zanesville, has a nice case on its high glaze and mat effects. Some of the "Old Copper" pieces are very good and look as if they had just been unearthed from the ruins of some ancient city."*

◆ ◆ ◆ ◆ ◆ ◆ ◆ ◆ ◆ ◆ ◆ ◆ ◆

Parchment Lotus

Introduced in 1906. Finished with a matt glaze with a "soft and wax-like luster." Decorated with flowers, animals, birds and fish." See Lotus for more information on the glaze. Although possibilities have been noted, this line has not been positively identified. No further information is available.

◆ ◆ ◆ ◆ ◆ ◆ ◆ ◆ ◆ ◆ ◆ ◆ ◆

Persian

Introduced in 1905.   The excerpt below is the only reference found so far to this line. There is no certainty this line was eventually named Persian, but there is also a possibility it was. No further information is available.

THE SOUTH-WESTERN'S BOOK - Vol. 2 - December 1905 - A visit to some Zanesville Potteries - by Lura Milburn Cobb. *"We were shown pieces of another new ware of odd shapes, and oriental in coloring and decoration, which is not yet on the market, and to which will probably be given the name of Persian ware."*

♦ ♦ ♦ ♦ ♦ ♦ ♦ ♦ ♦ ♦ ♦ ♦ ♦ ♦ ♦

Rainbow Bronze

Introduced in 1903. Listed in an Owens' advertisement in the October, 1903, issue of China, Glass and Pottery Review. No further information has been found, but the name would seem to indicate a rainbow colored bronze metallic coated piece. May be part of the Metal Deposit Line, only with coloring added.

♦ ♦ ♦ ♦ ♦ ♦ ♦ ♦ ♦ ♦ ♦ ♦ ♦ ♦

Red Flame

Introduced in 1905. Has an embossed floral design which is covered with a red glaze. May be marked with the line name. No further information is available.

Lotus

Introduced in 1906. Under-the-glaze slip painting, similar to Utopian but with lighter backgrounds. The background colors are often gray, grayish green, grayish blue, white, cream, pink, etc. or combinations thereof. Decorations are flowers, fish, scenes, birds, animals, etc. A 1907 advertisement describes Lotus, Brushmodel Lotus and Parchment Lotus as follows: "While in effect the lines are of mat finish, we have been fortunate in securing a most beautiful, soft and wax like lustre, which brings out in handsome relief the decorations." Also described as an "entirely new finish" and a "new process in finish." Although described as having a matt finish, this "new process matt finish" is only slightly softer to the touch and to the eye than the high gloss Utopian finish, and is easily mistaken for it. In all likelihood, the pieces shown here, all of which have been called "Lotus" for years by collectors, represent several different lines. The stork pieces, for example, may have been a separate line, and Items # 81 and # 88 may have been a line depicting small delicate flowers. And, of course, there are Brushmodel Lotus and Parchment Lotus, plus some pieces which have more of a standard matt finish. Unfortunately, at the present time, there is no definitive information available by which to positively sort out the possible different lines, and most light colored Owens pieces, unless already categorized, such as Alpine, will continue to be called "Lotus". Sometimes marked with the line name.

◆ ◆ ◆ ◆ ◆ ◆ ◆ ◆ ◆ ◆ ◆ ◆ ◆ ◆ ◆

CROCKERY AND GLASS JOURNAL - October 25, 1906 - Page # 27 - *"Other newcomers are fresh floral and bird studies on the Lotus ware."*

OPPOSITE PAGE

First Row
80. 4 7/8" Vase. Mark # 10. Shape # 231.
81. 5 7/8" Vase. Incised "Owens". Shape # 213.
82. 3 3/8" Vase with Mushrooms. Mark # 10. Impressed "Lotus". Shape # 202.

Second Row
83. 7½" Vase. Incised "Owens". Shape # 1258.
84. 10½" Vase. Torch Mark. "F" for Fouts. Shape # 1118.
85. 9 3/8" Pitcher with Fish. Mark # 10. Signed "Ferrell". Shape # 1212.
86. 9 3/8" Vase with Stork. Torch Mark. Shape # 1256.

Third Row
87. 12 7/8" Vase with Sailing Ship. Torch Mark. Unknown Artist. Shape # 1146.
88. 12 3/8" Pitcher with Pansies. Mark # 12. Shape # 1015.
89. 10 1/8" Vase with Pansies. Mark # 10. Shape # 1243.

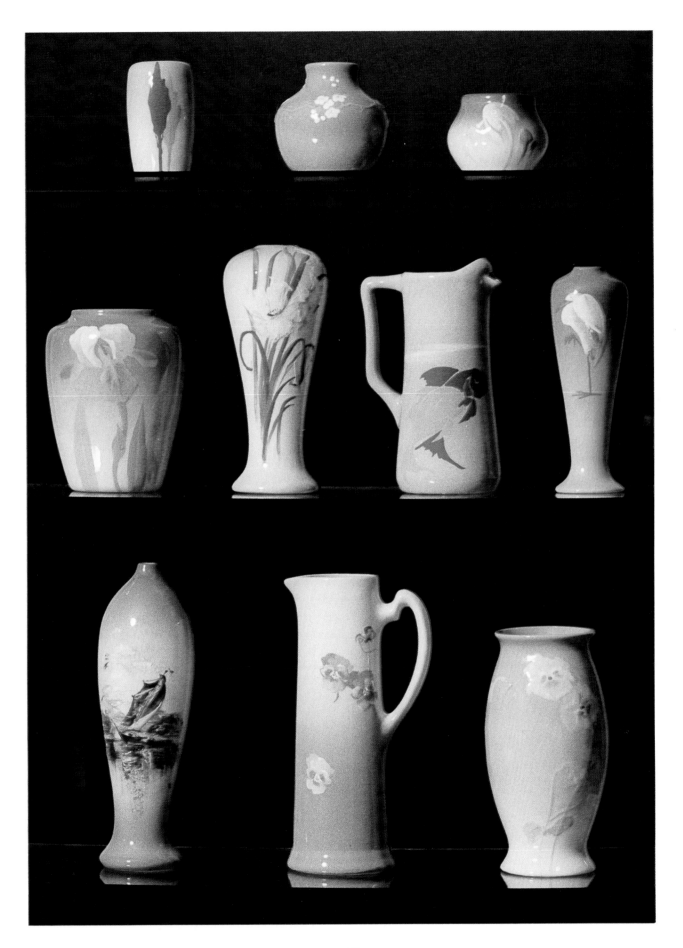

Lotus - Continued

90. 6¼" Vase. Marked "Owensart". Shape # 1177.
91. 14¼" Vase. Marked "Owens". Signed "A. F. Best". Shape # 1248.
92. 14½" Vase with Cranes in Flight. Torch Mark. Signed "Chilcote". Shape # 1251.
93. 14½" Vase with Wild Geese in Flight. Torch Mark. Signed "Chilcote". Shape # 1251.

 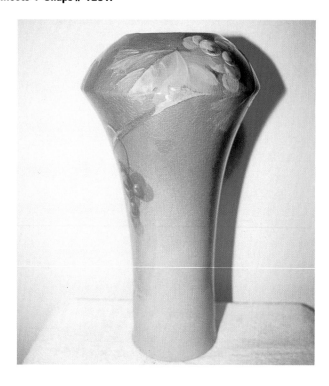

 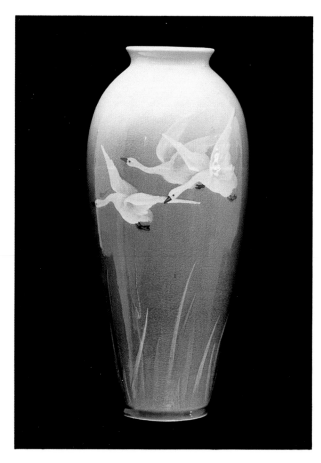

94.　10½" Vase. Markings Unknown. Signed "Chilcote". Shape # 1243.

95.　10 3/8" Vase with Pansies. Mark # 12. Shape # 010.

96.　14½" Vase with Fish. Torch Mark. Signed "Ferrell". Shape # 1252.

97.　10½" Vase with Fish and Sea Weed. Torch Mark. Signed "Ferrell". Shape # 1243.

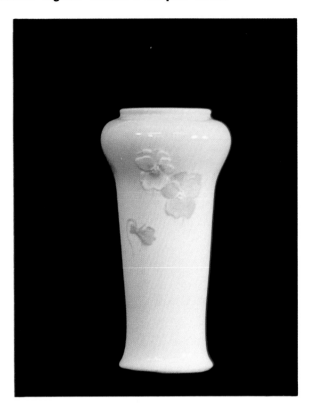

Lotus - Continued

First Row

98.   3¼" x 7" Teapot. Marked "Owens". By "Denny". Shape # 1255.

99.   6" Vase. Mark # 10. Impressed "LOTUS". Shape # 218.

100.   7 3/4" Vase with Water Lilies. Torch Mark. Shape # 1258.

SECOND ROW

101.   8" Vase. Torch Mark. Shape # 1258.

102.   10" Pitcher with Wading Bird. Markings Unknown.

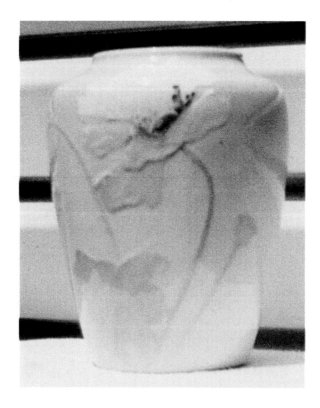

Lotus Line Pottery

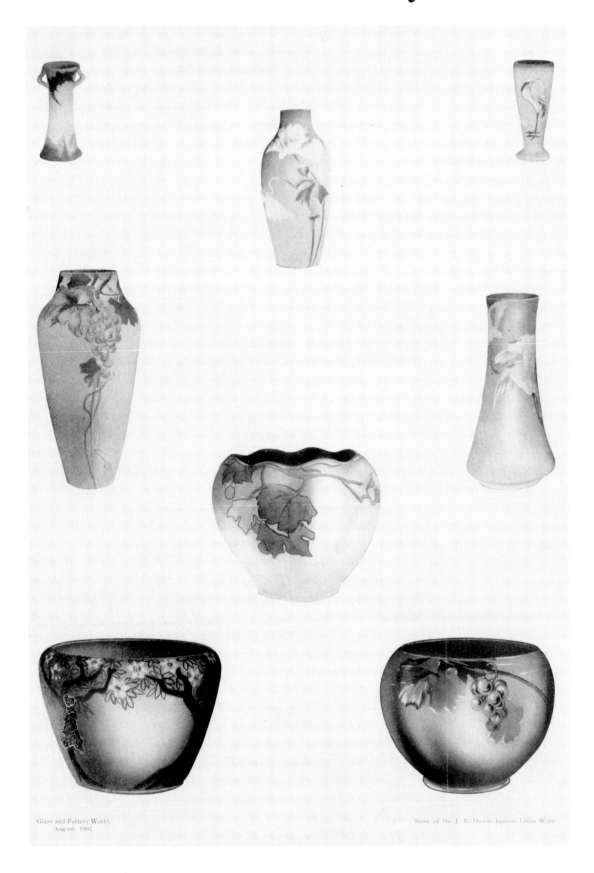

Glass and Pottery World.
August, 1907.

Some of the J. B. Owens famous Lotus Ware.

From the August, 1907, Issue of Glass and Pottery World.

Majolica Finish

Introduced in 1895. Has a majolica like high gloss finish. Discontinued in 1905. See Page 55.

See Page 55.

BELOW

First row

103.   31½" Jardiniere & Pedestal. Mark # 5.

104.   13½" Jardiniere. Mark # 5.

Second Row

105.   3 7/8" Long Green Paperweight. Mark # 5.

106.   3 7/8" Long Brown Paperweight. Mark # 5.

107.   11 5/8" Wall Pocket. Shape # 703.

OPPOSITE PAGE

First Row

108.   6½" Jardiniere. Mark # 1.

109.   3½" High Fern Dish. Mark # 1.

110.   6 7/8" Jardiniere. Mark # 1.

Second Row

111.   7½" Jardiniere. Mark # 1.

112.   7 3/4" Jardiniere. Mark # 1.

Third Row

113.   11" Jardiniere. Mark # 1.

114.   17½" Jardiniere and Pedestal. Mark # 1.

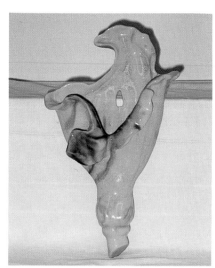

Matt Green

Introduced in 1905. Molded bodies, some smooth and some with embossed raised designs, in a matt green finish. Sometimes has the line name.

CROCKERY AND GLASS JOURNAL - February 22, 1906 - Page # 34 - *"Matt green forms a pleasing garb for wall pockets that have recently reached the J. B. Owens Pottery Co's showrooms. The pieces are fashioned in three different styles - ram's horn, cornucopia and bamboo. Their quiet coloring renders them more than ordinarily desirable as receptacles for cut flowers. Other of these hanging baskets are formed like the beet, acorn and squash. They, too, are clothed in matt green, as are also several shapes and sizes in jardinieres."*

BELOW
115.   11" Pitcher. Impressed "Owensart" and "Matt Green". Shape # 1109.
116.   5" Long Ashtray. Impressed "Owensart" and "Matt Green". Shape # 1107.

OPPOSITE PAGE
First Row
117.   5" Mug. Impressed "Owensart" and "Matt Green". Shape # 1108.
118.   5" Mug. Impressed "Owensart" and "Matt Green". Shape # 1215.
Second Row
119.   6" Vase. Unmarked. Shape # 1101.
120.   7 5/8" Vase. Impressed "Owensart" and "Matt Green". Shape # 1157.

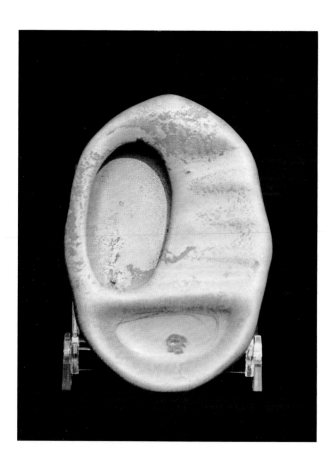

73

Matt Utopian

Introduced in 1902. Soft matt finish ware with pastel colored floral slip decorations of the Utopian type. Background colors are buff, dark brown and blue. Mostly marked Owens, and sometimes Owens Utopian. Have not seen a line name marked piece.

◆ ◆ ◆ ◆ ◆ ◆ ◆ ◆ ◆ ◆ ◆ ◆ ◆ ◆ ◆

CROCKERY AND GLASS JOURNAL - October 23, 1902 - Page # 19 - *THE NEW YORK TRADE - Conspicuous among W. H. Dunn's exhibit of the J. B. Owens Pottery Co.'s productions is the Utopian ware in a matt finish. Lacking the brilliancy of lustre possessed by their glazed counterparts, the matt-finished goods are nevertheless truly artistic. A kind of satin gloss relieves it from absolute dullness of color, and when surmounted by ingenious and tasty decorations it presents a very pleasing effect. The ware is shown in tankards, jugs, flower-holders, candlesticks and other like pieces.*

OPPOSITE PAGE

First Row

121.   5 3/4" Vase. Mark # 13. Shape # 112.

122.   5 7/8" Three Footed Pitcher. Mark # 13. "TS" for Tot Steele. Shape # 921.

123.   5¼" Footed Flat Vase. Mark # 13. "TS" for Tot Steele. Shape # 821.

124.   8" Vase. Mark # 13. "TS" for Tot Steele. Shape # 817.

Second Row

125.   9¼" Vase. Mark # 13. "HE" for Harriet Eberlein. Shape # 144 or # 1044.

126.   7" Three Handled Vase. Mark # 13. Artist Unknown. Shape # 826.

127.   6½" Jug. Mark # 13. Shape # 820.

Third Row

128.   12¼" Pitcher. Mark # 13 and "UTOPIAN". Shape # 1015.

129.   13" Vase. Mark # 13. "TS" for Tot Steele. Shape # 122.

130.   14 3/4" Vase. Mark # 13. Shape # 1067.

Matt Utopian - Continued

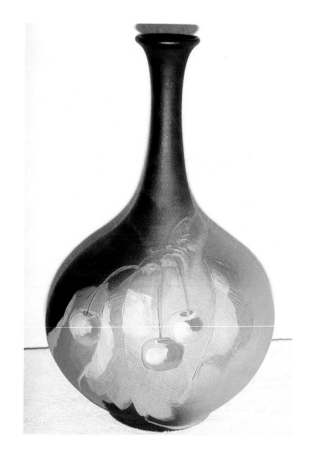

<u>BELOW</u>

131.　13" Blue Vase. Unmarked. Shape # 1055.

<u>Right Top</u>

132.　13¼" Vase with Cherries. Mark # 10. Impressed
　　　"UTOPIAN". "HE" for H. Eberlein. Shape # 1055.

<u>Right Bottom</u>

133.　20½" Umbrella Holder. Unmarked.

Metal Deposit (Deposit Metal)

Introduced in 1903. Listed in an Owens' advertisement in the October, 1903, issue of China, Glass and Pottery Review. This line has a pottery body which has an incised or slip-painted design over which metal has been electroplated so the design is still visible. Virtually identical to Clewell pottery. Two identically incised and shaped pieces, one marked "Owens" and the other marked "Clewell" have been seen. This would seem to indicate the pottery was made and incised by Owens who then sent it to Clewell, the metal coating expert. After electroplating it, Clewell, most likely, kept part, marked Clewell, for himself, and the other part, marked Owens, was sent back to Owens to be sold there. Have not seen a line name marked piece.

BELOW LEFT
134. 10" Gold Colored Vase. Marked "Owensart". Shape # 1060.

CENTER
135. 15" Incised Vase. Marked "Owensart". Shape # 1067.

TOP RIGHT
136. 5 3/8" Incised Vase. Marked "Owenzart". Shape # 115.

BOTTOM RIGHT
137. 6" Slip Decorated Vase. Marked "Owens". "C E" for Cecil Excel. Shape # 112.

Mission Pottery

Introduced in 1903. Characterized by mineral decorations in hand applied effects depicting old Spanish missions of the American Southwest. Each piece was accompanied by a stand or receptacle of "weathered oak" in keeping with the then-popular "Mission" style of decoration. Not all pieces have a mission on them. Some have a swirl design and others have an irregular design which looks like paint running down from the top. Sometimes marked with line name.

CHINA, GLASS AND LAMPS - January 16, 1903 - Page # 4 - *THE J. B. OWENS POTTERY CO. - "All you people who worship the antique and rail against the degeneracy of modern art must fall down on your knees before the old Mission pottery. That you have never seen anything in pottery that is more artistic you may be well assured. Nothing more original than the design and mounting has been introduced in pottery and it is little wonder if the old Mission marks an epoch in the potter's art."*

CHINA, GLASS AND POTTERY REVIEW - September 1903 - *"Mission pottery, a very beautiful and artistic adjunct to Mission furniture, is probably one of the very newest things in art pottery. The J. B. Owens Pottery Co., the sole manufacturers, are now exhibiting an excellent line of this pottery in their New York salesroom.*

On a visit to one of the prominent department stores in New York in search for ideas, and while viewing a display of Mission furniture, August W. Hutaf was struck with the glaring lack of harmony and inappropriate decorations which abounded about this particularly artistic furniture. To the average individual, there would have been nothing in the department's furnishing out of harmony, but what jarred the sensitive taste of the artist was the lack of bric-a-brac, china and pottery decorations that would harmonize with the mission furniture.

Mr. Hutaf asked himself, "Why can't I design pottery especially adapted for Mission furniture?". He began work earnestly, and after months of work given especially to the study of decoration, in order to produce a ware which would harmonize with Mission furniture, carefully selecting rich and subdued colors to comply with the scenery of lower California, where the Missions, now in stages of decay, exist, he submitted his ideas and designs to the J. B. Owens Pottery Co., of Zanesville, Ohio, in whose New York salesrooms and show windows can now be seen the result of his labors.

The colors are yellow, drab, various shades of green, garnet, etc. They are applied with a splash effect and finished in a dull glaze. Some are treated with a metallic antique luster finish, which tones down the colors even more than the dull glaze. The pottery is encased in a stand made of wood, which idea is taken directly from the Mission furniture. The clouds, moon, and sometimes the sun, in poster effect, finish the sky and background. The Mission houses stand out in quiet poses, and the lower parts of the pieces are treated in more subdued colors."

138. 10" (Estimated) Jardiniere in Wood Holder. Marked "Mission Pottery".

139. 12" Vase in Wood Holder. Unmarked.

140. 13 3/4" Splash Vase. Marked "Mission Pottery". Shape # 311.

141. 10½" Vase. Unmarked.

Mission Pottery - Continued

MISSION POTTERY FROM J. B. OWENS POTTERY CO.

DESIGNED BY AUGUST W. HUTAF.

The colors are applied with a splash effect and finished with a dull glaze. The Mission houses and other subjects stand out in quiet poses, and the lower parts of the pieces are treated in more subdued colors.

From the November, 1903, Issue of *China, Glass and Pottery Review.*

Monochrome Art

Introduced in 1906.   Listed in an Owens' advertisement in the February 22, 1906, issue of Crockery and Glass Journal as a new line of jardinieres. Pictured in the same advertisement, but not identified as Monochrome Art, is a jardiniere virtually identical to the one pictured below. This, plus the excerpt from the Crockery and Glass Journal, leads to an almost certain conclusion that the jardiniere pictured below is from the Monochrome Art Line. No further information is available.

CROCKERY AND GLASS JOURNAL - February 22, 1906 - Page # 34 - *"Handpainted designs on matt jardinieres and monochromatic brown, green and blue finishes on glazed "jars" are also among the new arrivals."*

<u>BELOW</u>
142.   7½" Jardiniere. Unmarked.

Onyx

Introduced in 1898. Pieces have mottled, striated and variegated designs of light, dark and medium brown, tan, gold, yellow, green, cream, red, etc., coloring. This line falls somewhere between majolica finish and art pottery. Identified by shape. Have not seen an Owens or a line name marked piece.

CHINA, GLASS AND POTTERY REVIEW - May 1898 - *J. B. Owens Pottery Co.   "We illustrate some pieces from the new line of colored high glaze pottery and Utopian lamps now being offered by this company. The onyx finish can be had in three colors - light, dark or medium."*

CHINA, GLASS & LAMPS - November 9, 1901 - Page # 9 - *AMONG ZANESVILLE ART POTTERIES. "Another pretty line is the onyx ware, comprising vases, umbrella stands, jardinieres, pedestals, fern bowls, tabourettes, etc. These goods are dark and yellow striped and resemble the tiger-eye ware. Like all the other products of this company, the pieces are gracefully modeled shapes and highly finished."*

BELOW
143.   5" Crescent Shaped Vase. Unmarked. Shape # 872.
144.   5" Jug. Unmarked. Shape # 790.
145.   4" Pillow Vase. Unmarked.

OPPOSITE PAGE
First Row
146.   7" Jug. Unmarked. Shape # 820.
147.   7" Jug. Unmarked. Shape # 820.
Second Row
148.   33" Jardiniere & Pedestal. Mark # 5.
149.   17" Pitcher. Mark # 8. Shape # 819.

Opalesce

Introduced in 1905. This ware has a gold background with an art nouveau style floral decoration in gold, silver, copper, or bronze outlined in black. Sometimes found with paper labels.

GLASS AND POTTERY WORLD - August 1905 - *"Opalesce Ware the Latest. As a result of long research and experimental work by the ceramic artists at the J. B. Owens Pottery Company, an entirely new ware has been put on the market. The critics in New York and at the Portland Exposition, where alone it has been shown, are so well impressed with its peculiar merit that it now looks as if the large outlay made by Mr. Owens would be repaid. The reputation of domestic pottery will be much enhanced when the Owensart opalesce ware becomes known. The first display was made in one of the most exclusive stores of Brooklyn and the art critics of the Eagle and Standard Union give unsolicited praise of the exquisite beauty of the ware and the extreme novelty of most of the shapes. The Opalesce line is the most ambitious effort of the progressive pottery and its creation represents a real innovation in the realm of the potter's art.*

Primarily the surface of the ware possesses the apparent metal quality of gold, both to the touch and sight. This body is almost hidden by colors most skillfully laid on. These shades are light, tending to greens, the golden body shining through in limited spaces. Intertwined through the ground colors are lines of contrasting colors giving a sort of mosaic effect. One side of each piece is occupied by an inlaid design of a floral character. The designs and the rather quiet tones utilized in their coloring suggest the Oriental or Grecian style of decoration."

BELOW
150. 18" Vase. Markings Unknown. Shape # 1125.
151. 10" Vase. Marked "Owens". Shape # 1124.

Opalesce Inlaid

Introduced in 1905. This ware has a gold background with an art nouveau style floral decoration in gold, silver, copper, or bronze outlined in black. In addition, it has a surface finish of a substance similar to small coraline-like beads surrounding the floral decoration. This ware is said to simulate the famous Italian Vermicel ware of the sixteenth century. Pieces of this line which have green beads are designated as Malachite (green) Opalesce Inlaid, so it is possible other pieces with different colored beads may have had special color names. Sometimes found with paper labels.

BELOW
152.   14" Vase. Unmarked.

TOP RIGHT
153.   8" Vase. Unmarked. Shape # 325.

154.   10 1/8" Vase. Unmarked. Shape # 1124.

BOTTOM RIGHT
155.   7 3/4" Vase. Unmarked. Shape # 1129.

Opalesce Utopian

Introduced in 1905. This ware was coated with gold and overlaid with small coraline-like beads excepting for one area which has an underglaze slip decoration. The slip decoration has the characteristics of the Utopian line. Pieces of this line which have green beads are designated as Malachite (green) Opalesce Utopian, so it is possible other pieces with different colored beads may have had special color names. Sometimes found with paper labels.

BELOW

First Row
156.   4 3/4" Vase. Mark # 13. Shape # 102.

Second Row
157.   11" Vase. Mark # 13. Shape # 1116 or # 1118.
158.   13" Vase. Mark # 13. Shape # 122.

BELOW

First Row

159.   5 3/4" Vase. Mark # 16. Shape # 112.

160.   6½" Jug. Mark # 13. Shape # 820.

161.   7 3/4" Vase. Mark # 13. Shape # 1069.

162.   5" Humidor. Unmarked.

Second Row

163.   12 7/8" Vase. Mark # 13. Shape # 124.

164.   13 3/8" Vase. Mark # 13. Shape # 128.

165.   13" Vase. Mark # 10. Shape # 1068.

166.   12 3/8" Pitcher. Mark # 13. Shape # 1015.

Oriental

Introduced in 1898. Squeeze bag decorated in small beads of light colors on dark backgrounds. The beads are flat on the surface while Cyrano, another Owens' line, is similar, but with some of the decoration raised off the surface. Practically identical to Weller's Turada. Often marked with the line name.

CROCKERY AND GLASS JOURNAL - July 14, 1898 - Page # 14 - *THE NEW YORK TRADE - "W. H. Dunn is showing some new lamps in Oriental ware. The goods are in raised, beaded effects in light colors on dark backgrounds. The same ware is shown in jardinieres."*

OPPOSITE PAGE

First Row

167.   4 3/4" Miniature Jardiniere. Impressed Mark # 9 and "Oriental". Shape # 701.

168.   2 3/8" Bowl. Mark # 9.

Second Row

169.   7 3/8" Ewer. Unmarked.

170.   6 3/8" Three Footed Vase. Unmarked.

171.   5 5/8" Four Footed Flat Vase. Mark # 8. Shape # 821.

Third Row

172.   6¼" Jug. Impressed Mark # 9 and "Oriental". Shape # 758.

173.   10½" Vase. Unmarked. Shape # 823.

174.   5¼" Jug. Unmarked. Shape # 790.

Oriental - Continued

BELOW

First Row
175.   5" Crescent Footed Vase. Unmarked. Shape # 872.
176.   4¼" Four Footed Flat Vase. Unmarked.

Second Row
177.   7 3/8" Mug. Mark # 9 and "Oriental". Shape # 830.
178.   11¼" Vase. Unmarked. Shape # 863.

Poster

Introduced in 1900. Decorated with figures of actors and musicians. Background and glaze similar to Utopian. Sometimes marked with the line name.

CROCKERY AND GLASS JOURNAL - January 29, 1903 - Page # 29 - *THE NEW YORK TRADE* - *"An artistic addition to the window display of the J. B. Owens Pottery Co. has just been made at their West Broadway salesrooms. It is a line of Poster ware, which, as the name implies, is patterned after the color ideas suggested by the odd poster effects that first attracted general attention at the Paris Exposition. The decorations are slightly raised above the surface of the ware - a process that lends additional life and spirit to the figures. Despite the originality and oddity in the blending of colors, there is withal a harmony that is quite artistic."*

BELOW

179.   11" Vase with Wagner Portrait. Marked "J. B. Owens" and "Utopian". "A.W. Williams". Shape # 1010.

Rustic

Introduced in 1904. A line of jardinieres, window boxes, planters, vases, etc., shaped to resemble sections of trees. Owens' ads state "Most perfect imitation of wood ever produced." From this, it would seem the pieces would have a brown or dark brown coloring, however, the pieces found in rustic shapes are of semi-glossy green. Have not seen a line name marked piece.

CROCKERY AND GLASS JOURNAL - June 2, 1904 - Page # 13 - *"That ever-original concern, the J. B. Owens Pottery Co., have just opened for observation samples of an imitation rustic wood effect that is remarkable in its similitude to nature. The bark is formed and raised in such a finished manner, and the coloring bears such a striking resemblance to the wood from which it is copied, that an observer is liable to be deceived unless he touches the piece. The line embraces jardinieres and pedestals designed for the lawn, cemetery, park or veranda, umbrella stands, hanging baskets and window boxes."*

CROCKERY AND GLASS JOURNAL - August 10, 1905 - Page # 15 & # 16 - *"One of the largest pieces of pottery ever produced in this country reached the J. B. Owens Pottery Co.'s salesrooms on Monday. It is an adjunct of the rustic wood line, and is as faithful in modeling and coloring as the smaller specimens. The piece is imitative of a portion of a large tree that has been sawed off at either end. It stands five feet six inches in height, measures twenty inches in diameter, and weighs about seven hundred pounds."*

BELOW

180. 6½" Vase. Marked "Owensart".
181. 9¼" Vase. Marked "Owensart".

Semi-Glazed Etched

Introduced in 1906. Listed in an Owens' advertisement in the February 22, 1906, issue of Crockery and Glass Journal, and described below in an article from the same magazine. Have not seen a line name marked piece.

CROCKERY AND GLASS JOURNAL - March 22, 1906 - Page # 30 - *"From the J. B. Owens Pottery Co. have just come hand-etched vases that further evidence the spirit of progressiveness in the sphere of art pottery. The design itself is carved out by hand. The carved outlines are accentuated by the application of white coloring and the design is treated either in light blue, brown or other tints that make it fairly stand out from the body of the ware. The subjects employed are usually of a floral character, although symbolical of modern art ideas in the matter of form and coloring rather than closely imitative of nature."*

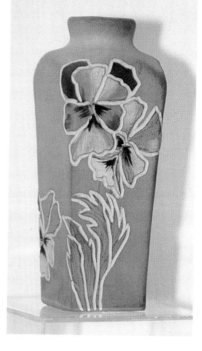

RIGHT
182.   6" Vase. Marked "OWENSART. Shape # 112.

BELOW
183.   16¼" Vase. Mark # 16. Shape # 782.
184.   7 3/8" Vase. Mark # 10. Shape # 128.
185.   13 1/8" Vase. Mark # 13. Shape # 123.

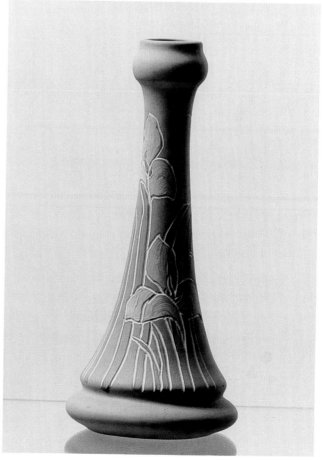

Silver Overlay Utopian and Lightweight

Introduced in (?). Utopian ware overlaid in fancy designs with sterling silver. Also included here are Utopian pieces with silver plated attachments.

RIGHT

186. 13½" Lightweight Pillow Vase. Mark # 8. "John Herold". Shape # 788.

BELOW

First Row

187. 3¼" Vase. Mark # 14. Shape # 862.

188. 3 5/8" Ewer. Mark # 14. Shape # 922.

189. 3¼" Twist Vase. Mark # 10. Shape # 101.

190. 7 1/8" Double Handled Lightweight Vase. Incised "JBO". By "Cecil Excel".

191. 8 3/8" Double Handled Lightweight Vase. Mark # 14. Shape # 884.

Second Row

192. 3 Piece Tea Set with Silver Plated Attachments. Mark # 9. Shape # 1057.

193. 5" Vase. Marked "J. B. Owens" and "Utopian". Shape # 944.

Soudaneze (Soudanese)

Introduced in 1907. An ebony black matt glazed ware with pastel colored slip decorations in shades of pearl, lavendar and white. Decorated with flowers, fish, etc. Although Soudaneze was designated as being "Matt" glaze, it is possible this is the same type "Matt" glaze introduced in 1906 on the Lotus line. In other words, a high gloss matt glaze. Accordingly, Soudaneze comes in two finishes: A high gloss matt finish, and a true matt finish which is smooth and satin-like similar to the art vellum finish. Sometimes marked with the line name.

GLASS AND POTTERY WORLD - June 1907 - *"The Soudanese line is of ebony black in matt glaze, with decorations in light color effects."*

BELOW
194.   12" Glossy Vase. Unmarked. Shape # 221.

Top Right
195.   4 3/4" Glossy Vase. Mark # 3. Shape # 211.
196.   8½" Glossy Vase. Mark # 10 and "Soudaneze". Shape # 220
197.   4 5/8" Glossy Vase. Unmarked. Shape # 200.

Bottom Right
198.   5¼" Matt Vase. Mark # 10. Shape # 212.

Sunburst

Introduced in 1906. A brown Utopian-type ware with a high-gloss glaze finish using brighter colors, including a light gold highlighting blend of darker gold, russet and yellow for the slip painted decorations. Similar to Weller's Aurelian. Sometimes marked with the line name.

BELOW
199.   16" Tankard. Incised "J. B. Owens" and "Sunburst". "A. H." for Albert Haubrich. Shape # 819.

TOP RIGHT
200.   5½" Jug. Mark # 8. "Excel" for Cecil Excel. Shape # 790.

BOTTOM RIGHT
201.   6" Jug. Mark # 9 and "Utopian". Shape # 793.

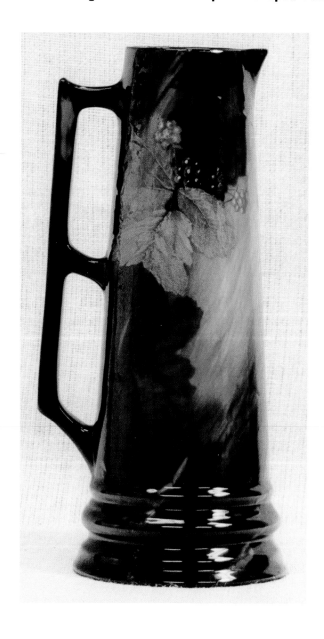

Sylvan Green

Introduced in 1906. - A dark green matt line embossed with foliage, trees, flowers, etc. in a "Romanesque" style. Have not seen a line name marked piece.

CHINA, GLASS AND LAMPS - April 7, 1906 - Page # 5 - *"and we believe it will be pronounced the closest reproduction of that most beautiful color of nature's verdure." A representative of China, Glass and Lamps was shown a sample of this ware, it was placed beside the ordinary or accepted green color line, and he unhesitatingly says that the contrast was so great that this old piece looked like a dull-shade of pale blue."*

CHINA, GLASS AND LAMPS - May 5, 1906 - Page # 6 - *"Sylvan Green" is the name of the new line of the J. B. Owens Pottery Co., which Sales Manager Geo. Brush says has started off with a rush.*

CROCKERY AND GLASS JOURNAL - May 17, 1906 - Page # 15 - *"Many additions have been made during the past few days to the J. B. Owens Pottery Co.'s "Romanesque" Sylvan matt green vases. The forms, as the name suggests, are of a Roman style, embodying massiveness of outlines with artistic proportions. The sizes run from three to sixteen inches."*

BELOW
202.   10 3/8" Pitcher. Mark # 10. Shape # A12.
203.   12 1/8" Vase. Unmarked.

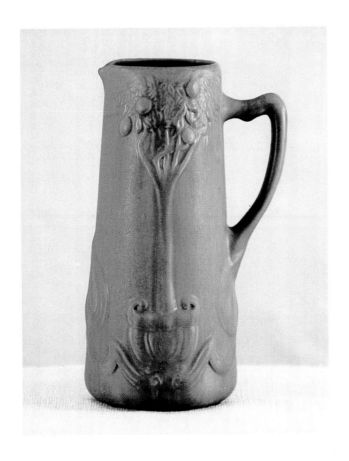 

Tile

Starting in 1905, Owens made tile under the name of the Zanesville Tile Company. In subsequent years he made tile under the names of the Zanesville Floor and Wall Tile Company, the J. B. Owens Floor and Wall Tile Company, the Empire Floor and Wall Tile Company, and, perhaps, others. Often marked with the company name.

BELOW

First Row
204. 12" Square Nursery Rhyme Tile. Marked "EMPIRE".
205. 11 3/4" Square Tile with Sailboat. Marked "OWENS".

Second Row
206 5 3/4" Square Green and White Border Tiles. Marked "OWENS".
207. 5 15/16" Square Tulip Tile. Marked "OWENS".
208. 3" Square Decorative Tiles. Marked "EMPIRE".
209. 4 1/8" Square Decorative Tile. Marked "EMPIRE".
210. 5" Square Decorative Tile. Marked "EMPIRE".

Transfer*

Introduced in 1903. These high-glaze pieces are decorated with transfers (decals) of animals, Indians, women, etc. on colored backgrounds. Have seen jardinieres and pedestals with Indians, dogs, and women on them. Sometimes marked Owens. Have not seen a line name marked piece.

CROCKERY AND GLASS JOURNAL - May 21, 1903 - Page # 16 - *THE NEW YORK TRADE - "There is a tankard set from the J. B. Owens Pottery Co. at W. H. Dunn's warerooms that is quite new and shown in three distinct styles of color treatment. One is a salmon ground with an Indian's head as the decoration; another has a female head on an apple-green ground; the third also shows a feminine head, but on a sky-blue ground."*

BELOW
211. 12 3/8" Tankard Pitcher. "No Neck Chief". Mark # 13. Shape # 1015.

TOP RIGHT
212. 5 1/8" Mug. Unmarked. Shape # 1035.
213. 5¼" Mug. Unmarked. Shape # 1035.

BOTTOM RIGHT
214. 5 1/8" Mug. Unmarked. Shape # 1035.
215. 5 1/8" Mug. Mark # 10. Shape # 1035.

Unidentified As to Line

All of the pieces pictured here are Owens. Some may belong to lines already listed in this book, but could not be positively identified with enough certainty to place them there. Others are undoubtedly from lines about which information has not yet been found.

<u>**BELOW**</u>

<u>**First Row**</u>

216.   4 3/4" Mug. Unmarked. Shape # 1108. Embossed "TAKE THE YELLOW OUT". (Feroza Shape)

217.   6 1/8" Vase. Torch Mark. Shape # 1155B.

<u>**Second Row**</u>

218.   10¼" High Gloss Vase. Lightly Incised Decoration. Owens Shape.

219.   17" Vase. Fancy Squeeze Bag Decoration. Torch Mark. Shape # 1181. (Persian Line?)

220.   9" Vase with Squeeze Bag Decoration. Incised "Owens".   By "Ferrell".
221.   6 3/4" Vase. Mark # 10. Shape # 0225. (See Piece # 49)

Second Row
222.   13" Pitcher with Lady's Portrait. By "Cora McCandless". Shape # 1015.
223.   13" Vase with Squeeze Bag Decoration. Torch Mark. Shape # 1178. (Persian Line?)

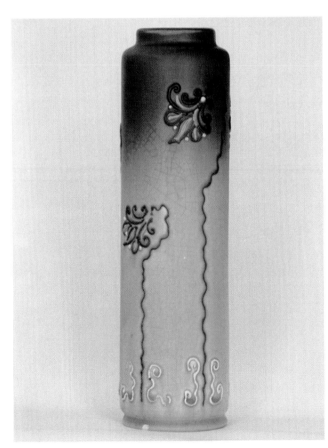

Unidentified As to Line - Continued

224. 18 3/4" Vase with Squeeze Bag Decoration. Torch Mark. Shape # 1180.

225. 8" Matt Finish Vase. Unusual Decoration. Mark # 10. Shape # 220.

226. 10½" Red Glaze Vase. Marked "Owens". "FF" for Frank Ferrell. Shape # 1060. (Red Flame?)

227. 10" Matt Incised Vase. Mark # 16. In the style of Frederick H. Rhead. Shape # 1010.

228. 4¼" Vase with Slightly Embossed Dragonflies. Marked "Owens". Shape # 201.

229. 7 1/8" Handled Vase. Mark # 10. Shape # 1161.

230. 7 1/8" Vase. Mark # 13.

231. 10 3/4" Vase. Torch Mark. Shape # 1203. (Multi-Blend?)

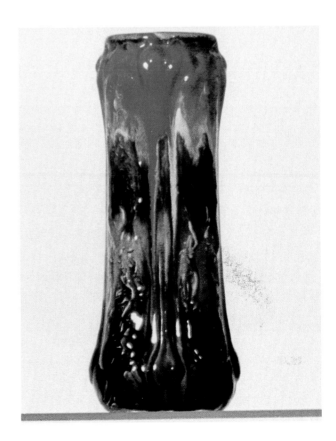

Unidentified As to Line - Continued

232. 7" Vase. Mark # 10. Shape # 32.

233. 2¼" Lucky Pig Bank. Unmarked. (Owens made a line of novelty banks).

234. 5¼" Vase. Mark # 10. Shape # 29.

235. 5 5/8" Vase. Mark # 12. Shape # 50.

Exclusive
Designs

OUR SPECIALTY

J. B. OWENS'
VASES OF QUALITY

Jugs, Jardinieres, Lamps, Stands
and Portables

If we haven't what you want
we will make it.   Write us.

J. B. OWENS
ZANESVILLE, OHIO, U. S. A.

Owens' Advertisement

Utopian

Introduced in 1896. Originally made on seal brown backgrounds, but later made in shades of blue, green, pink, brown, gray, etc. An underglaze slip-painted high gloss finish ware decorated with portrait heads of American Indians, horses, dogs, cats, etc., as well as floral designs. The turquoise blue background was brought out in 1900, and the blended backgrounds in 1901. See descriptions of the blended backgrounds below. Often Marked Owens and Utopian.

◆ ◆ ◆ ◆ ◆ ◆ ◆ ◆ ◆ ◆ ◆ ◆ ◆ ◆

CROCKERY AND GLASS JOURNAL - January 10, 1901 - Page # 28 - *THE NEW YORK TRADE* - "W. H. Dunn has just received a lot of new goods from the J. B. Owens Pottery Co. which include besides new decorations in Utopian ware, an entirely new line in light colors. A specimen piece is in pearl grey, shading to pink and green, with a heavy dark brown which is almost a black at top and bottom. For ornament a well-excecuted cat's head stands out with striking effect."

◆ ◆ ◆ ◆ ◆ ◆ ◆ ◆ ◆ ◆ ◆ ◆ ◆ ◆

CROCKERY AND GLASS JOURNAL - July 18, 1901 - Page # 13 - *THE NEW YORK TRADE* - "The "Utopian" is brought out in effects in light colors this season. There are light grays with pink or peach tints, greens, and blues intermingled as grounds, with artistic painting superimposed."

OPPOSITE PAGE

First Row

236.   10 5/8" Horse Portrait Vase. Mark # 9, and "Utopian". "M.T." for Mae Timberlake. Shape # 1010.

237.   13 3/8" Sleepy Kittens Pillow Vase. Mark # 14 and "Utopian". "M.T." for Mae Timberlake. Shape # 788.

Second Row

238.   15¼" Cat Portrait Vase. Marked "Owensart" and "Utopian". "H E" for Hattie Eberlein. Shape # 1039.

239.   8½" Dog Portrait Vase. Mark # 14 and "Utopian". Signed "C. L. Leffler". Shape # 1037.

107

Utopian - Continued

BELOW

240.   6¼" Vase with Whippet. Mark # 9 and "Utopian". "HE" for Hattie Eberlein. Shape # 1116.

241.   4" Pillow Vase with Kitten. Mark # 9 and "Utopian". "MT" for Mae Timberlake. Shape #1051.

OPPOSITE PAGE

First Row

242.   10½" Vase with Kittens. Marked "J. B. Owens". "Mae Timberlake". Shape # 1010.

243.   15 3/8" Vase with Dog. Mark # 16. Shape # 1039.

Second Row

244.   16" Vase with Chicks. Mark # 14. "MT" for Mae Timberlake. Shape # 1078.

245.   11½" Footed Pillow Vase with Dogs. Marked "Owens". Signed "A. Haubrich 1900". Shape # 1013.

Utopian - Continued

BELOW

246.   14 3/4" Vase with Indian Portrait.   Unmarked.   "Weasaw Shoshone".   "MTS" for Mary Fauntleroy Stevens. Shape # 1067.

247.   11 7/8" Vase with Indian Portrait. Mark # 9. "Weasaw Shoshone". Signed. Shape # 1038.

OPPOSITE PAGE

First Row

248.   11½" Vase with Indian Portrait. "High Bear Sioux". Mark # 9. "EBP" for E. B. Pitser. Shape # 1052.

249.   12" Vase with Indian Portrait. Note American Flag in Headdress. "M. Timberlake". Shape # 1052.

Second Row

250.   24" Umbrella Stand. "The Man - Assinboines". Signed "A. Williams". Shape # 1058.

251.   16" Vase with Indian Portrait. Markings Unknown. Shape # 1039.

111

Utopian - Continued

BELOW

252.   12" Vase with Man Golfer. Marked "J. B. Owens - Utopian". "AFB" for A. F. Best. Shape # 1025.

253.   11¼" Vase with Woman Golfer. Mark # 9. Signed "E. B. Pitser". Shape # 1052.

OPPOSITE PAGE

First Row

254.   20" Vase with Indian Portrait. "Chief Josh Apache". Signed "A. Williams 1901."

255.   14" Vase with Portrait of a Shepard. Marked "J. B. Owens". "AFB" for Anna Fulton Best. Shape # 1116.

256.   13" Pillow Vase with Gypsy Girl Portrait. "Anna Fulton Best". Shape # 788.

257.   19 5/8" (With Shade) Lamp. Unmarked. Shape # AS11.

Utopian - Continued

BELOW

258.   12" Pillow Vase with Horse Portrait. Marked "Owens". Shape # 1013.

259.   15 3/4" Vase with Grapes. Mark # 9 and "Utopian". Signed "A. Haubrich 1901". Shape # 899.

OPPOSITE PAGE

First Row

260.   13" Vase with Biblical Figure. Marked "Owens". Signed "C. L. Leffler". Shape # 1038.

261.   13" Pillow Vase with Portrait. Mark # 14. Signed "A. F. Best". Shape # 1013.

Second Row

262.   13" Blue Tankard. Marked "J. B. Owens" and "Utopian". Signed "S. Timberlake". Shape # 1015.

263.   5" Blue Mug. Mark # 10. "TS" for Tot Steele.

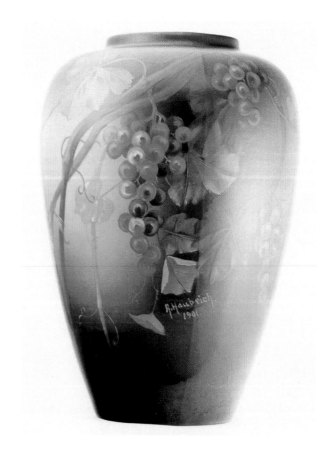

Utopian - Continued

OPPOSITE PAGE

First Row
264. 2" Planter. Mark # 9. "HR" for Harry Robinson.
265. 3¼" Vase. Mark # 9. Shape # 862.
266. 3 7/8" Vase. Mark # 9. Shape # 109.
267. 3 3/4" Vase. Mark # 10. Shape # 111.
268. 3½" Vase. Mark # 10. Shape # 105.
269. 3 7/8" Vase. Mark # 10. "CD" for Cora Davis. Shape # 113.
270. 2 5/8" Vase. Mark # 10. "CD" for Cora Davis. Shape # 103.

Second Row
271. 3 3/8" Twisted Vase. Mark # 10. Shape # 101.
272. 3 3/4" Vase. Mark # 10. Shape # 116.
273. 4½" Twisted Vase. Mark # 10. Shape # 117.
274. 4 7/8" Three Sided Vase. Mark # 10. Shape # 120.
275. 4 1/8" Vase. Mark # 10. Shape # 1110.
276. 3" Vase. Mark # 7. Shape # 1270.

Third Row
277. 5½" Vase. Mark # 12. Shape # 232.
278. 4 3/4" Vase. Mark # 10. Shape # 213.
279. 4½" Stein. Mark # 10.
280. 5" Vase. Mark # 10. Shape # 1080.
281. 5 1/8" Footed Flat Vase. Mark # 15. "F" for Charles Fouts. Shape # 821.
282. 6½" Vase. Mark # 9. "TS" for Tot Steele.

Fourth Row
283. 5" Stein. Mark # 13. Shape # 1035.
284. 5 5/8" Footed Vase. Mark # 9.
285. 6" Vase. Mark # 9. Shape # 928.
286. 5 3/4" Jug. Mark # 14. Shape # 967.
287. 5 7/8" Vase. Mark # 10. Shape # 108.
288. 4" Vase. Mark # 14. Shape # 978.

Fifth Row
289. 3½" Handled Vase. Mark # 9. Shape # 936.
290. 4¼" Footed Vase. Mark # 14. "RH" for Roy Hook. Shape # 931.
291. 4 7/8" Tan Colored Vase. Mark # 9. "DH" for Delores Harvey. Shape # 975.
292. 6" Vase. Mark # 10. Shape # 112.
293. 4 7/8" Twisted Vase. Mark # 10. Shape # 102.
294. 4" Handled Vase. Mark # 9. Shape # 980.

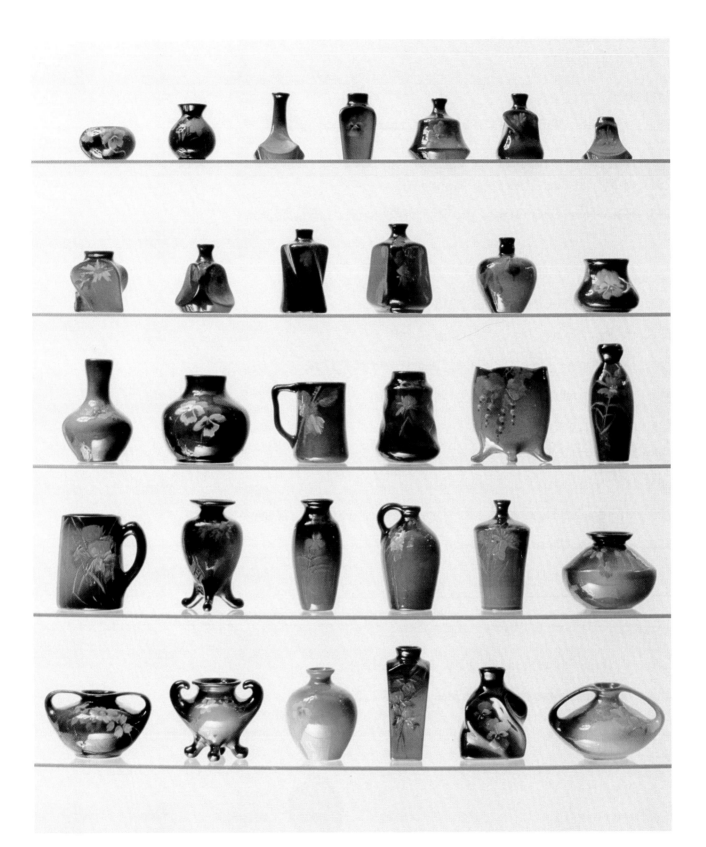

Utopian - Continued

OPPOSITE PAGE

First Row

295. 7½" Vase. Mark # 9. "MT" for Mae Timberlake. Shape # 1069.

296. 6 3/4" Jug. Mark # 7. Shape # 820.

297. 6 1/8" Tan Jug. Mark # 13. Shape # 793.

298. 5½" Footed Ewer. Mark # 10. "TS" for Tot Steele. Shape # 921.

Second Row

299. 6" Vase. Mark # 10. Shape # 218.

300. 5" Handled Jug. Mark # 13. Shape # 790.

301. 3½" Planter. Mark # 7. Signed "Denny". Shape # 1253.

302. 7 1/8" Handled Jug. Mark # 7. Shape # 820.

Third Row

303. 9½" Vase. Mark # 9. Shape # 1044.

304. 10" Handled Ewer. Mark # 9. Signed "A. Haubrick 1901". Shape # 1053.

305. 10" Vase. Unmarked. Shape # 1118.

306. 9¼" Vase. Mark # 7.

Fourth Row

307. 4" Three Footed Vase. Mark # 9. Shape # 938(?).

308. 4½" Footed Crescent Shaped Vase. Mark # 9. Shape # 872.

Utopian - Continued

OPPOSITE PAGE

First Row

309.   8 3/4" Vase. Mark # 10. "CD" for Cora Davis. Shape # 126.

310.   10 7/8" Vase. Mark # 13. Signed "B. Mallen". Shape # 1073.

311.   9¼" Vase with Pears. Mark # 10. Shape # 259.

312.   10¼" Vase with Cherries. Mark # 13. "IS" for Ida Steele. Shape # 1060.

313.   8 3/8" Vase. Mark # 7.

Second Row

314.   10 3/8" Vase. Mark # 12. Shape # 03.

315.   8" Vase. Mark # 14. Shape # 817.

316.   10½" Vase. Mark # 10. Shape # 01.

317.   8 1/8" Vase. Mark # 9. Shape # 227.

318.   10½" Vase. Mark # 10. Shape # 08.

Third Row

319.   11 3/8" Vase. Mark # 10. Shape # 1290.

320.   12½" Vase. Mark # 11. Shape # 014.

321.   13 5/8" Vase. Mark # 13. Shape # 015.

322.   10½" Vase. Mark # 11. Shape # 05.

323.   10¼" Vase. Mark # 13. Shape # 1010.

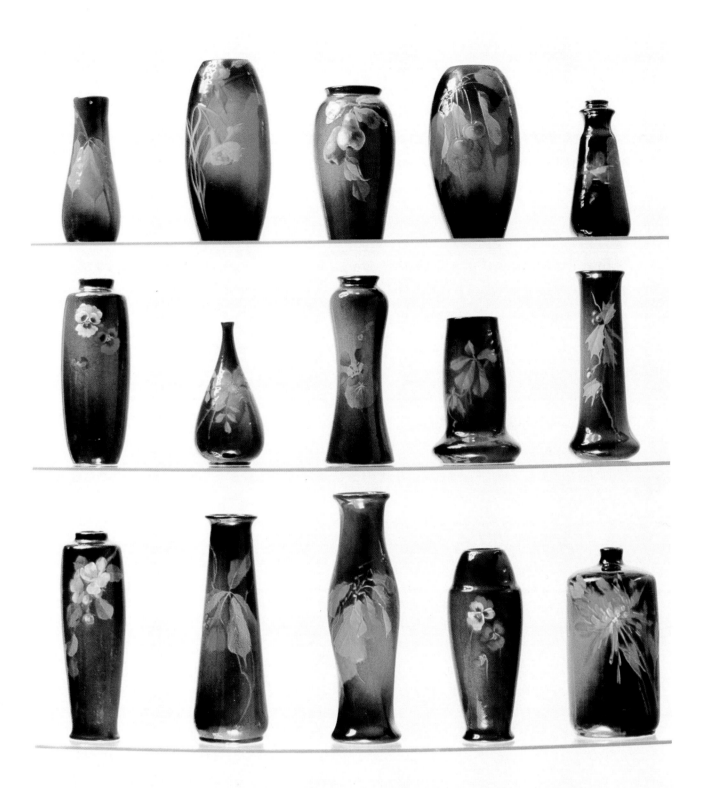

Utopian - Continued

OPPOSITE PAGE

First Row

324.   3 3/4" Footed Ewer. Mark # 14. Shape # 921(?).

325.   3 7/8" Footed Ewer. Mark # 9. Shape # 922.

326.   4 7/8" Vase. Mark # 12. Shape # 238.

327.   5 7/8" Twisted Vase. Mark # 10. Shape # 115.

Second Row

328.   7¼" Handled Jug with Corn. Mark # 10. "TS" for Tot Steele. Shape # 1266.

329.   7" Three Handled Loving Cup with Cherries. Mark # 13. "HE" for Hattie Eberlein. Shape # 826.

330.   6¼" Vase. Mark # 9. Shape # 1114.

331.   7" Stein. Mark # 14. Shape # 830.

Third Row

332.   12¼" Pitcher. Mark # 10. Shape # 1015.

333.   15" Vase. Mark # 10. Shape # 1067.

334.   12 3/4" Vase with Cherries. Mark # 13. Shape # 1076.

Utopian - Continued

BELOW

335.   12" Vase. Mark # 10. Shape # 1055.
336.   12" Vase. Mark # 9. Shape # 1055.

OPPOSITE PAGE

First Row
337.   5¼" Vase with Kitten Portrait. Mark # 14. Shape # 1048.
338.   6 5/8" Vase with Indian Portrait. Mark # 9. "Weasaw, Shoshone". "MFS" for Mary Fauntleroy Stevens. Shape # 820.
339.   5" Lightweight Vase with Bees. Mark # 9. Artist Signed. Shape # 805.

Second Row
340.   7 1/8" Humidor with Playing Cards, etc. Mark # 12. Shape # 1017.
341.   7 1/8" Humidor with Smoking Items. Mark # 10. Shape # 1017.

Third Row
342.   18" Vase. Marked "Owens". Shape # 216.
343.   7 7/8" Green Utopian Vase. Mark # 13. Shape # 1129.

Venetian

Introduced in 1903. This ware features a dark colored metallic glaze with an iridescence intensified by the depressions or elevations on its irregular surface. The iridescence resembles oil floating on water. Has been seen with the line name design painted under the glaze, and, also, with a paper label.

CROCKERY AND GLASS JOURNAL - July 23, 1903 - Page # 23 - *THE NEW YORK TRADE* - *"Venetian ware" is this week being exhibited for the first time in the West Broadway display windows of the J. B. Owens Pottery Co. There is a high lustre to the ware that invests it with the characteristics of metal rather than clay. Iridescent colors form the decoration, both interiorly and exteriorly. The line includes vases only."*

RIGHT

344.   5½" Double Handled Vase. Marked "Venetian".

Bottom Row

345.   9½" Diameter Double Handled Vase. Paper Label with "Venetian".

346.   9 1/8" Double Handled Vase. Unmarked.

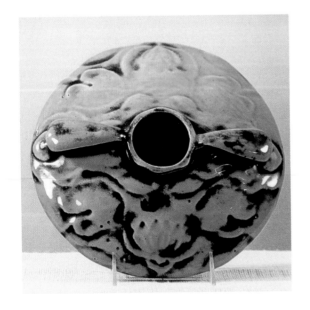

Owens Advertisement

Index to
Black and White Pictures and Illustrations

Advertisements 15, 22, 26, 32, 105, 122, 127

Aqua Verdi Vase 38

Corona Animals 43

Corona Line Statue 41

Delft Line Tub 46

Factory in 1895 7

Factory in 1901 7

Jeweled Line Vase 54

Lotus Line Pottery 69

Majolica Finish Pottery Illustrations 55

Mission Pottery 80

New York City Salesroom Exterior 8

New York City Salesroom Interior 8

Owens' Picture 9

Salesman's Business Card 15